Gastric Sleeve Cookbook

The Ultimate Guide to Taking Care Of Your New Stomach, with Bariatric Recipes to Avoid Regaining Weight after Surgery. 40-Day Meal Plan Included

By

Charles Rueson

© Copyright 2023 by Charles Rueson - All rights reserved.

This document is geared towards providing exact and reliable information regarding the topic and issue covered. The publication is sold with the idea that the publisher is not required to render accounting, officially permitted or otherwise qualified services. If advice is necessary, legal or professional, a practiced individual in the profession should be ordered.

From a Declaration of Principles which was accepted and approved equally by a Committee of the American Bar Association and a Committee of Publishers and Associations.

In no way is it legal to reproduce, duplicate, or transmit any part of this document in either electronic means or printed format. Recording of this publication is strictly prohibited, and any storage of this document is not allowed unless with written permission from the publisher. All rights reserved.

The information provided herein is stated to be truthful and consistent in that any liability, in terms of inattention or otherwise, by any usage or abuse of any policies, processes, or Instructions contained within is the solitary and utter responsibility of the recipient reader. Under no circumstances will any legal obligation or blame be held against the publisher for reparation, damages, or monetary loss due to the information herein, either directly or indirectly.

Respective authors own all copyrights not held by the publisher.

The information herein is offered for informational purposes solely and is universal as such. The presentation of the data is without a contract or any guarantee assurance.

The trademarks used are without any consent, and the publication of the trademark is without permission or backing by the trademark owner. All trademarks and brands within this book are for clarifying purposes only and are owned by the owners themselves s, not affiliated with this document.

Table of Contents

Introduction 8

Chapter 1: Basics of Sleeve Gastrectomy 9
   Stage 1: Liquids 10
   Stage 2: Purees 11
   Stage 3: Soft Foods 12

Chapter 2: Liquid Recipes 16
   1. Celery Juice 16
   2. Fresh Vegetable Broth 17
   3. Sugar-Free Ginger Tea 19
   4. Mint Tea 20
   5. Decaf Iced Coffee 21
   6. Pineapple Infused Water 22
   7. Cranberry Apple Juice 23
   8. Lemon Cucumber Detox Water with Mint 24
   9. Sugar-free Banana Popsicles 25
   10. Strawberry Lemon Infused Water 26

Chapter 3: Breakfast Recipes 27
   11. Blueberry Breakfast Pancakes 27
   12. Cottage Cheese Breakfast Bowl 28
   13. Scrambled Eggs with Cottage Cheese 29
   14. Banana Muffins 30
   15. Egg Salad 31
   16. Tuna and Spinach Pancakes 32
   17. Baked Eggs with Greens and Beans 33
   18. Apple Cinnamon Porridge 35
   19. Strawberry Avocado Smoothie 36
   20. Green Vegetable Fritters 37
   21. Apple Cheese Strudel 38
   22. Vegetable Breakfast Bakes 40
   23. Fat Burning Smoothie 41

24. Chia Pudding 42

25. Cranberry and Raspberry Smoothie 43

Chapter 4: Vegetable Recipes 45

26. Mushroom Alfredo Cauliflower Gnocchi 45

27. Cauliflower Pizza Crust 46

28. Mushroom Risotto 48

29. Vegetable Lasagna 49

30. Stuffed Peppers 51

31. Pan Quesadilla with Jalapeno Ranch 52

32. Vegetarian Chili 54

33. Stir Fry Tofu with Peanut Sauce 56

34. Vegetarian Meatballs 57

35. Tofu Lettuce Wraps 59

36. Creamy Zucchini Pasta 60

37. Green Curry Buddha Bowl 62

38. Burrito Bowl with Crema 63

39. Garlic and Seasame Ramen Noodles 65

4o. Cauliflower Taco with Avocado Crema 66

Chapter 5: Seafood Recipes 68

41. Seafood Enchiladas 68

42. Shrimp and Corn Succotash 70

43. Rosemary Salmon with Potatoes and Asparagus 71

44. Shrimp and Cauliflower Bake 73

45. Fish and Shrimp Stew 74

46. Panko and Parmesan Crusted Scallops 76

47. Clam Chowder 77

48. Crab Louie Salad 78

49. Pita Bread Salmon Sandwich 80

50. Balacao Guisado 81

51. Walnut Rosemary Salmon 82

52. Korean Grilled Mackerel 83

53. Tuna, White Bean and Dill Salad 84

54. Fish Curry 86

55. Shrimp Piccata with Zucchini Noodles 87

Chapter 6: Meat and Poultry Recipes 89

56. Birria 89

57. Beef Stroganoff	90
58. Creamy Tuscan Chicken	91
59. Gyro Meat	93
60. White Sauce Breast Chicken	94
61. Beef and Broccoli Stir Fry	96
62. Meatloaf with Vegetables	97
63. Spinach and Turkey Lasagna	98
64. Chicken Pot Pie	100
65. Paleo Tomato Chicken Curry with Cauliflower Rice	102
66. Tandoori Chicken	103
67. Shiitake Mushroom Chicken Ramen	105
68. Pumpkin Chilli Chicken	106
69. Stuffed Chicken Breast	108
70. Creamy Mushroom Chicken	110

Chapter 7: Dessert Recipes	**111**
71. Black Bean Fudge Brownies	111
72. Zucchini Double Chocolate Bread	112
73. Chocolate Tahini Cookies	114
74. Oatmeal and Peanut Butter Cookies	115
75. Sweet and Sour Potato Muffins	116
76. Chai Tea Glaze with Pumpkin Spice Bundtlettes	118
77. Avocado Brownies with Frosting	119
78. Fluff Cake	121
79. Vegan Chocolate Pudding	122
80. Chocolate Baked Donuts	123
81. Strawberry Ice cream	125
82. Chocolate Truffles	126
83. Chocolate Amaretti	127
84. Chocolate Covered Strawberries	128
85. Greek Yogurt Brownies	129

Chapter 8: Snack Recipes	**131**
86. Guacamole with Bell Pepper Dippers	131
87. Cottage Cheese with Fruit	132
88. Celery Sticks with Cream Cheese	132
89. Cucumber with Hummus	133
90. Olives with Feta Cheese	134
91. Roasted Chickpeas	135

- 92. Turkey Roll-Ups ... 136
- 93. Hard Boiled Eggs ... 137
- 94. Apple with Peanut Butter ... 138
- 95. Carrot Chips ... 139

BONUS 1: 40-Day Meal Plan ... 141

- Day 1 ... 141
- Day 2 ... 141
- Day 3 ... 141
- Day 4 ... 141
- Day 5 ... 142
- Day 6 ... 142
- Day 7 ... 142
- Day 8 ... 142
- Day 9 ... 143
- Day 10 ... 143
- Day 11 ... 143
- Day 12 ... 143
- Day 13 ... 144
- Day 14 ... 144
- Day 15 ... 144
- Day 16 ... 144
- Day 17 ... 145
- Day 18 ... 145
- Day 19 ... 145
- Day 20 ... 145
- Day 21 ... 146
- Day 22 ... 146
- Day 23 ... 146
- Day 24 ... 146
- Day 25 ... 147
- Day 26 ... 147
- Day 27 ... 147
- Day 28 ... 147
- Day 28 ... 148
- Day 29 ... 148
- Day 30 ... 148
- Day 31 ... 148

Day 32 148
Day 33 149
Day 34 149
Day 35 149
Day 36 149
Day 37 149
Day 38 150
Day 39 150
Day 40 150

Conclusion 151

BONUS 2 - Handy Conversion chart 153

Introduction

The surgical treatment known as a sleeve gastrectomy causes weight loss by limiting food intake. The surgeon removes roughly 75% of the stomach during this treatment, which is typically done laparoscopically. As a result, the stomach begins to resemble a sleeve and can only hold a little amount of food. According to statistics, this treatment has been shown to reduce weight by up to 65% of the excess weight; better outcomes are attained with nutritional and behavior adherence. Patients who have undergone sleeve gastrectomy will benefit from and sustain successful weight loss with wise food choices, consistent exercise, and healthy eating habits.

The dangers of gastric sleeve surgery are significantly smaller than the hazards of obesity and its associated disorders. Additionally, it has fewer complications than other common procedures like hip replacement and gallbladder surgery. The majority of gastric sleeve operations are carried out using minimally invasive surgical methods, which results in less discomfort from incisions and a quicker recovery.

Once an individual goes through this surgery, a two-week liquid diet will come after the health screening. Individuals will be given detailed instructions to follow by their surgeon. In order to make the procedure safer, it is intended to shed part of the belly and liver fat. Before the procedure, patients won't be allowed to eat or drink anything for 12 hours. This is to ensure that the stomach is empty when the treatment begins. Having food or drink in the stomach while undergoing surgery may have unfavorable or even harmful side effects.

To make sure that the stomach heals properly in the near future, one must adhere to strict food restrictions. One might start eating more normally after a few months but should still need to make informed dietary choices. Patient needs to make sure that what they do eat is nutritious enough to meet daily energy demands because they won't be able to consume as much as one is used to. Soon after surgery, one should start taking vitamins, and they need to do so indefinitely.

Gastric sleeve surgery provides good weight loss and health advantages, even though the average weight loss is a little less than with more advanced weight loss procedures. The main point for the surgery to work is for the patient to follow a low-calorie diet that will help them loose weight as well as stay healthy in the meantime. In the following chapters are recipes that patients can follow to lose weight after gastric sleeve surgery. So let's dive into it!

Chapter 1: Basics of Sleeve Gastrectomy

People who are healing after sleeve gastrectomy also known as gastric bypass, are given the opportunity to rehabilitate and to change their eating habits with the assistance of a gastric bypass diet.

A doctor or a trained dietitian will talk a person through the diet they will need to follow post-surgery. They will explain what kinds of food one can consume at each meal as well as how much one can eat overall. If one wants to reduce weight in a healthy way, following their gastric bypass diet to the letter can assist.

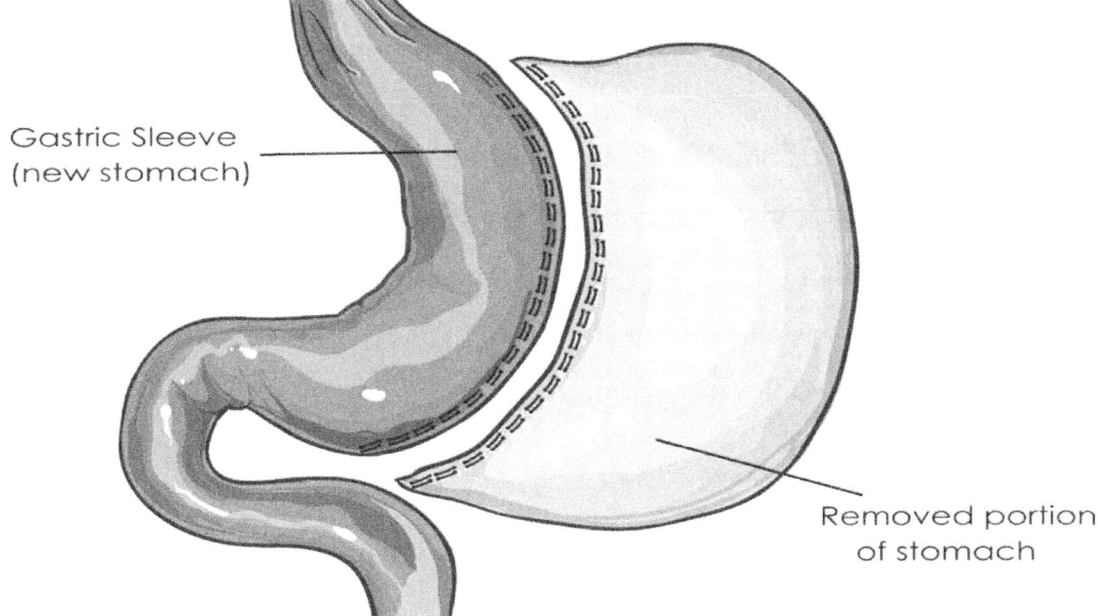

Dietary modifications in gastric bypass are intended to:

Give the stomach a chance to mend without being restricted by the expansion caused by eating. One should become used to consuming reduced amounts of food that the reduced stomach can easily and carefully digest. This will reduce weight and prevent them from gaining weight in the future.

Dietary advice following gastric bypass surgery is highly variable and should be tailored to each patient's unique circumstances. The gastric bypass diet often utilizes a phased approach in order to assist patients in gradually transitioning back to eating solid foods. How quickly users progress from one stage to the next is determined by how quickly the body recovers from the previous step and adjusts to the new eating patterns. About three months after surgery, patients will often be able to resume eating their regular diet.

At each and every step of the gastric bypass diet, one needs to make sure that they pay special attention to prevent themselves from being dehydrated and aim to consume 64 ounces of fluid per day. They should drink liquids in between meals rather than at the same time as meals. Drinking anything for at least half an hour before a meal is not recommended, and a person should wait at least that long after eating before drinking anything. Eating and drinking carefully can help one avoid the dumping syndrome, which is likely to occur when the meals and fluids enter the small intestine quickly and in bigger amounts than typical. Symptoms of dumping syndrome include nausea, vomiting, dizziness, excessive perspiration, and diarrhea.

Consumption of Food After Gastric Sleeve Surgery.

After the surgery is performed, one should make sure to pick out foods and beverages that are low in sugar and fat. They should avoid alcohol at any cost. Caffeine, which can lead to dehydration, should be consumed in moderation. Patients should always make sure to follow their doctor's orders when it comes to taking dietary supplements, including vitamins and minerals.

After the patient goes through the surgery, they will be restricted to drinking only clear liquids for the first day or so after the procedure. After they have gained some experience with clear liquids, they will be ready to go on to additional liquids such as:

Stage 1: Liquids

Following are the liquids that one can consume post gastric sleeve surgery.

- Unsweetened Juices
- Coffee or tea (without the caffeine)

- Milk
- Popsicles
- Sugar-free gelatin
- Purred Foods

Stage 2: Purees

After the patient has been able to tolerate liquids for about a week, they can start eating meals that have been strained and pureed (also known as mashed up). The meals should have the consistency of a thick liquid or a smooth paste, and there should be no chunks of solid food in the mixture. The patient should strive to consume three to six smaller meals per day. Four to six teaspoons of food should make up each meal that they eat. They should consume each meal over a period of approximately half an hour.

Following are the items that can be pureed easily:

- Ground lean meat, poultry or fish, or both
- Eggs are prepared in a gentle scrambling style.
- Cooked soft fruits and vegetables
- Cereals that have been cooked.
- Cream soups that have been strained
- Cottage cheese

Combine liquids with solid foods, such as the following:

- Water Skim milk
- Sugar-free Juice
- Broth
- Chewable foods

Stage 3: Soft Foods

After a few weeks of eating just pureed foods, and with the approval of one's physician, the patient can transition to eating soft foods. They should be bite-sized portions of food that are soft, sensitive, and easy to chew. Users should strive to consume three to five smaller meals per day. One-third to one-half of a cup of food should make up the entirety of each meal. Before swallowing, thoroughly masticate each bite of food until it has the consistency of mush.

These are examples of soft foods:

- Lean ground meat or ground poultry
- Cottage cheese
- Cereal, either cooked or dried
- Eggs made from flaked fish
- Rice
- Fruit that has been canned or is tender and fresh.
- Foods that are not liquids
- Cooked Vegetables

After following the gastric bypass diet for around eight weeks, one will be able to slowly transition back to eating foods that have more texture. To get started, try eating three meals a day, with one cup to one and a half cups worth of food comprising each meal. It is vital to quit eating before one feels as though one cannot possibly fit another bite in. One may be able to adjust the number of meals they eat per day as well as the amount of food they consume at each meal according to how well they handle solid food. One should have a discussion about what's best for them with their nutritionist.

After gastric bypass surgery, eating certain meals could result in discomfort, nausea, or vomiting. The following types of foods have the potential to be problematic at this stage:

- Breads
- Foods that have been fried
- Beverages
- Seeds and nuts both.
- Raw veggies
- Fibrous vegetables
- Foods that are
- Dishes that are extremely seasoned or hot
- Popcorn

With the passage of time and the physician's supervision, one may eventually be able to consume some of these foods once more.

Following surgery, it is essential to take in sufficient nutrients while ensuring progress toward the desired weight loss. One of the medical providers will likely advise them to:

- Consume food and liquids gently. To prevent dumping syndrome, one should give themselves at least thirty minutes to eat each meal and between thirty and sixty minutes to drink one cup of liquid. If they want to consume liquids before or after each meal, hold off for half an hour.

- Keep meals small. Consume a number of smaller meals throughout the day. One could begin by eating six little meals each day, then gradually work their way down to four meals, and then settle on three meals per day following a standard diet. One should consume approximately a half cup to a full cup's worth of food at each meal.

- Drink liquids between meals. An individual needs to consume at least 8 cups, or 1.9 liters, of fluids on a daily basis to keep from becoming dehydrated. However, consuming excessive fluids before, during, or after a meal can cause one to feel excessively full and prevent them from eating enough food that is high in nutrients.

- Be sure to chew one's food completely. It is possible for larger pieces of food to obstruct the new aperture that runs from the stomach into the small intestine because it is rather thin. Blockages prohibit food from being expelled from the stomach and can lead to nausea, vomiting, and pain in the abdominal region. Eat the food in manageable chunks, chew it thoroughly until it reaches puree consistency, and then swallow it.

- Focus on foods that are strong in protein. Consume these foods before eating any of the other foods that are included in the meal.

- Steer clear of foods that are heavy in both sugar and fat. These foods create dumping syndrome because they move through the digestive tract quickly.

- Take the vitamin and mineral supplements that have been suggested. After surgery, the body will be unable to properly digest and absorb the nutrients from the food they eat. It is highly possible that one will have to continue taking a multivitamin supplement on a daily basis for the rest of their life.

Results of Gastric Sleeve Surgery

One may speed up the recovery following surgery and make a smoother transition to a way of eating that is both healthy and supportive of the efforts to lose weight when one follows the gastric bypass diet. Keep in mind that if one goes back to the old unhealthy eating habits after having weight-loss surgery, it is possible that they may not lose all of the weight that they need to lose or that they will gain back any weight that they do lose.

Risks of Gastric Sleeve Surgery

The most significant dangers associated with the gastric bypass diet arise from improper adherence to the eating plan. They could run into problems if they eat more than they should or if they consume foods that they shouldn't. These are the following:

- Dumping syndrome: If an excessive amount of food enters the small intestine in a short amount of time, they may have symptoms including nausea, vomiting, dizziness, excessive perspiration, and diarrhea. After a meal, feeling sick to the stomach or throwing up can be caused by several factors, including eating too much or too quickly, consuming foods heavy in fat or sugar, and not chewing the food thoroughly enough.

- Dehydration: Some people become dehydrated because they break the rule that says one shouldn't drink anything with the meals. Because of this, one should drink a total of 64 ounces or 1.9 litres of fluids throughout the course of the day, including water and other beverages.

- Constipation: Constipation can be caused by not getting enough exercise, fiber, or liquids in the diet, as well as not moving around enough.

- Obstructed entrance of the pouch in the stomach: Even if one adheres to the diet extremely strictly, food can become stuck at the opening of the stomach pouch. Ongoing nausea, vomiting, and abdominal pain are some of the signs and symptoms of an obstruction in the stomach opening. If one has these symptoms for more than two days, one should make an appointment with a primary care physician.

- Gaining weight or being unable to sustain a loss of weight: Talk to the primary care physician or a registered dietitian if, after following the gastric bypass diet, one finds that they are unable to lose weight or continue to gain weight.

Chapter 2: Liquid Recipes

1. Celery Juice

Prep Time: 3 minutes

Cook Time: 11 minutes

Servings: 4

Ingredients:

- 1 lime, skin removed
- 2 stalks of celery

Instructions:

1. In order to prepare the celery for juicing, begin by chopping off the bottoms of the stalks and the tips of both bunches of celery.
2. Put the celery stalks in a colander and put the colander in the sink. After washing it, the celery should be patted dry.
3. Place the lime and celery into the juicer's feeding tube and begin juicing.
4. Serve the juice immediately, store any excess in a container that seals tightly, and place it in the refrigerator. Consume the juice within three days of making it.

Nutritional Info:

Calories: 83 kcal Fat: 0.1 g Protein: 1.3 g Carbs: 21.9 g Sugar: 14.4 g Sodium: 40.4 mg

2. Fresh Vegetable Broth

Prep Time: 30 minutes

Cook Time: 1 hour 30 minutes

Servings: 4

Ingredients:

- 1 teaspoon sea salt, optional
- 2 tablespoons olive oil
- 1 to 2 cups of leftover vegetable scraps
- 12 cups of water
- 3 fresh sprigs of thyme
- 3 medium onions
- 4 cloves of garlic, crushed and peeled
- 4 Small Tomatoes
- 5/4 ribs of chopped celery
- 5/6 Medium Carrots
- 1/2 an ounce of dried mushrooms,
- A bunch of fresh parsley
- A pair of bay leaves

Instructions:

1. Heat oven to 425 degrees F. To roast the vegetables, one will need a baking sheet with a rim or a baking dish measuring 9 inches by 13 inches.
2. The onion should be peeled and then roughly chopped into pieces no larger than 1 inch. Carrots and celery should be thoroughly scrubbed before slicing into around 1-inch bits. After being washed, cut the tomatoes in half or quarters, depending on their size.
3. Put the garlic, onion, carrots, and celery on a baking sheet or pan, and then add the tomato. After tossing them with olive oil, roast the vegetables for fifteen minutes. Roast for another 15

minutes after stirring the vegetables. After giving it one more stir, put it back in the oven for another ten minutes until the veggies are golden brown and the tomatoes begin to collapse.

4. Place the dried mushrooms in a bowl, cover them with approximately a half cup of cold water, and leave them aside for about five minutes.

5. Transfer the roasted vegetables to a deep stockpot using a spoon. After adding one cup of water to the baking tray or pan, give it a good stir while scraping the bottom to remove as many of the browned bits that have adhered to it as possible. Pour on top of the veggies that are currently located in the stockpot.

6. Add the thyme, parsley, bay leaves, and leftovers of vegetables that need to be used up in addition to the salt (if using).

7. After adding the mushrooms that have been partially rehydrated, strain the water that they have been sitting in through a filter with a fine screen to remove any grit. Add the mushroom water that has been filtered to the saucepan that contains the veggies.

8. Just before serving, cover with 11 glasses of water. Bring to a boil, then lower the heat to keep it going. Cook for 45 minutes with the lid only partially on.

9. After straining the broth, one can use it right away, store it in the refrigerator for up to three days, or freeze it for up to three months. Once one is ready to use it, give the broth a taste and adjust the seasoning as necessary by adding more salt or, if one doesn't mind using fish sauce, a few dashes of it.

Nutritional Info:

Calories: 70 kcal Fat: 3 g Protein: 2 g Carbs: 10 g Sugar: 5 g Sodium: 40.4 mg

3. Sugar-Free Ginger Tea

Prep Time: 5 minutes

Cook Time: 10 minutes

Servings: 2

Ingredients:

- 1/4 cup lemon juice
- 14 of a cup of honey
- 1 lemon (sliced)
- 1 piece of ginger
- 1 ounce of water.
- 3 bags of black tea
- 18 to 20 pieces of cubed ice

Instructions

1. Bring the water to a boil in either a saucepan or a pot.
2. In a large mug, combine tea sachets and ginger. The mug should be filled with scalding hot water.

3. After submerging the tea bags in the liquid several times, steep the tea for ten minutes.
4. Take out the tea bags, then stir in the honey and lemon juice. Combine thoroughly.
5. Place ice cubes and a few slices of lemon in each of the two glasses. Douse the ice cubes with the piping hot tea. Mix well and serve.

Nutritional Info:

Calories: 141 kcal Fat: 3 g Protein: 2 g Carbs: 33 g Sugar: 35 g Sodium: 17 mg

4. Mint Tea

Prep Time: 2 minutes

Cook Time: 5 minutes

Servings: 2

Ingredients:

- Honey
- ½ pack of mint

Instructions:

1. Take a few mint leaves in one hand and clap the palm of the other hand on top of the first hand while simultaneously dropping the mint leaves into a teapot or coffee pot. Repeat with the remaining mint, making sure to set aside a couple of sprigs of mint to decorate the top of each glass.
2. Fill the kettle with boiling water and let the tea steep for about two to three minutes, or until the color of the liquid begins to change to a very light yellow or green. After the tea has been strained, pour it into mugs or heat-resistant glasses and add honey to taste.

Nutritional Info:

Calories: 13 kcal Fat: 0 g Protein: 0.1 g Carbs: 3 g Sugar: 35 g Sodium: 0 mg

5. Decaf Iced Coffee

Prep Time: 5 minutes

Cook Time: 5 minutes

Servings: 1

Ingredients:

- 1 tsp warm water
- 1 tsp vanilla extract (optional)
- 2 teaspoons of decaffeinated granules of instant coffee
- 1/2 cup of ice-cold water
- 1/2 cup of the milk
- 1 cup of ice cubes
- Honey (optional)

Instructions:

1. Blend decaffeinated coffee granules with hot water until the granules are completely dissolved. This is the method for making decaffeinated iced coffee.
2. Stir or blend the mixture until smooth after adding the sugar, cold water, and vanilla extract (if using).

3. After filling a tall glass with ice cubes, pour the coffee mixture on top of the ice.

4. Add milk to one's liking. Serve with honey (optional).

Nutritional Info:

Calories: 180 kcal Fat: 9 g Protein: 2 g Carbs: 13 g Sugar: 26 g Sodium: 30 mg

---

6. Pineapple Infused Water

Prep Time: 5 minutes

Cook Time: 5 minutes

Servings: 2

Ingredients:

- 4 cups of freshly cut-up pineapple pieces
- 4 tablespoons of white sugar
- 4 cups of ice-cold water

Instructions:

1. Cube the pineapple and set it aside.

2. Put the four cups of pineapple chunks and one or two glasses of water into a blender. Blend until smooth.

3. Blend until smooth, making sure that all of the pieces are included.

4. After straining the mixture into a bowl, transfer the pineapple water to a larger container. If one wants the pulp to remain in the beverage, one should skip this step.

5. The final portions of water and sugar should be added. Combine thoroughly.

6. Try it out, and if it needs it, add additional sugar or water.

7. Enjoy a sip over some ice!

Nutritional Info:

Calories: 130 kcal Fat: 0 g Protein: 1 g Carbs: 35 g Sugar: 29 g Sodium: 2 mg

7. Cranberry Apple Juice

Prep Time: 5 minutes

Cook Time: 2 minutes

Servings: 2

Ingredients:

- 1/4 teaspoon of lemon zest (grated)
- 2 teaspoons of fresh ginger
- 1/2 cup of water
- 1 cup raw apple juice
- 2 cups of frozen cranberries

Instructions:

1. Put all of the ingredients into the blender, and then process them on high speed for thirty to sixty seconds or until the mixture is smooth and creamy.

Nutritional Info:

Calories: 133 kcal Fat: 0.3 g Protein: 0 g Carbs: 27 g Sugar: 16 g Sodium: 7 mg

8. Lemon Cucumber Detox Water with Mint

Prep Time: 5 minutes

Cook Time: 5 minutes

Servings: 1

Ingredients:

- 1 glass of water
- ½ cup of ice cubes (optional)
- 1-2 lemons (sliced)
- 3-4 mint leaves
- 6-7 cucumber slices (cut into round slices)

Instructions:

1. Take a jar of any kind, whether it be a water jar or a mason jar.
2. Slice some cucumbers and add them to it.
3. Mix in some lemon segments cut into rounds.
4. Add mint leaves.
5. After that, stir in the water.
6. Put the cover back on.
7. Place in the refrigerator for two hours so that the flavors may fully develop.
8. To make it a colder beverage, add ice cubes and serve chilled.

Nutritional Info:

Calories: 145 kcal Fat: 3 g Protein: 11 g Carbs: 20 g Sugar: 26 g Sodium: 35 mg

9. Sugar-free Banana Popsicles

Prep Time: 5 minutes

Cook Time: 4 hours

Servings: 12

Ingredients:

- 2 tablespoons honey
- 4 bananas, medium-sized
- 12 cups of milk
- Cinnamon vanilla extract (optional)
- Powdered cocoa (optional)

Instructions:

1. Blend all of the ingredients together until smooth in the food processor, then add the optional ingredients as preferred.
2. Pour the mixture into the molds, making sure to leave a little room at the top for the candy to grow. Insert sticks, then freeze the mixture until it is solid
3. After running the mold under warm water for a few seconds to release the ingredients, remove the ingredients from the mold.

Nutritional Info:

Calories: 61 kcal Fat: 0.4 g Protein: 0.9 g Carbs: 14 g Sugar: 9.8 g Sodium: 6 mg

10. Strawberry Lemon Infused Water

Prep Time: 10 minutes

Cook Time: 10 minutes

Servings: 4

Ingredients:

- 1 large lemon, sliced
- 1 cup of fresh strawberries
- 4 cups of water

Instructions:

1. Put some strawberry slices and lemon slices into a pitcher. The natural tastes of the fruit need to be released into the water, so use the back of a spoon or a muddler to gently muddle it.
2. Cover with the filtered water, then place in the refrigerator for at least a day's worth of time.
3. Enjoy this refreshing drink by pouring it over ice in a glass and garnishing it with a slice of lemon and a strawberry.

Nutritional Info:

Calories: 23 kcal Fat: 0 g Protein: 1 g Carbs: 7 g Sugar: 3 g Sodium: 7 mg

Chapter 3: Breakfast Recipes

11. Blueberry Breakfast Pancakes

Prep Time: 15 minutes

Cook Time: 20 minutes

Servings: 3

Ingredients:

- 1 teaspoon of baking powder
- 200g of self-rising flour
- 300 ml of milk
- 1 cup of blueberries
- 1 cup of butter
- 1 egg
- 1 bottle of maple syrup
- 1 bottle of sunflower oil

Instructions:

1. In a sizable bowl, combine 200g of self-rising flour, 1 teaspoon of baking powder, and a dash of salt.

2. Making a hole in the middle of the dry ingredients, whisk in the milk to create a thick, smooth batter. Beat 1 egg with 300 ml of milk.

3. Gently fold in half of the package of blueberries after adding a knob of melted butter.

4. In a sizable non-stick frying pan, heat a teaspoon of oil or a small knob of butter.

5. For each pancake, add a generous tablespoon of the batter, resulting in pancakes. At a time, make 3 or 4 pancakes.

6. Small bubbles should develop on the surface of every pancake after about 3 minutes of cooking time over medium heat. Turn the pancakes over and cook for an additional 2-3 minutes or until golden.

7. While using the remaining batter, keep it warm by covering it with kitchen paper.

8. Serve with the remaining blueberries and golden or maple syrup.

Nutritional Info:

Calories: 108 kcal Fat: 3 g Protein: 4 g Carbs: 18 g Sugar: 0 g Sodium: 4 mg

12. Cottage Cheese Breakfast Bowl

Prep Time: 2 minutes

Cook Time: 3 minutes

Servings: 1

Ingredients:

- 1/2 teaspoon vanilla extract (optional)
- 1/2 tablespoon of chia seeds
- 1 1//2 tablespoons of almonds
- 1/2 cup of fat-free Greek yogurt
- 1/2 cup of cottage cheese
- 1 ounce of fresh strawberries
- Cinnamon powder (optional)

Instructions:

1. Place the cottage cheese and yogurt in a bowl and mix them together.

2. Add some chia seeds, almonds, and berries to the top of the bowl.

3. If one prefers, one can top it with some cinnamon and drizzle some vanilla over it.

Nutritional Info:

Calories: 328 kcal Fat: 14.4 g Protein: 30 g Carbs: 17 g Sugar: 10 g Sodium: 946 mg

13. Scrambled Eggs with Cottage Cheese

Prep Time: 5 minutes

Cook Time: 5 minutes

Servings: 2

Ingredients:

- 1 teaspoon of ground black pepper
- 1 teaspoon of freshly chopped chives (Optional)
- 1 tablespoon of butter
- 1/4 cup of cottage cheese
- 4 big beaten eggs

Instructions:

1. In a skillet set over medium heat, melt the butter. Pour the beaten eggs into the skillet and leave them alone to cook for 1 to 2 minutes or until the bottom of the eggs starts to set up.

2. Add black pepper to the mixture after adding cottage cheese and chives. Cook and stir for a further 3 to 4 minutes or until the eggs are almost set.

Nutritional Info:

Calories: 224 kcal Fat: 17 g Protein: 16 g Carbs: 2 g Sugar: 1 g Sodium: 295 mg

14. Banana Muffins

Prep Time: 10 minutes

Cook Time: 20 minutes

Servings: 12

Ingredients:

- 1/2 teaspoon of baking soda
- 1/2 teaspoon of vanilla extract
- 1/8 teaspoon of salt
- 1-tablespoon baking powder
- 1/4 cup of apple sauce
- 1 cup of flour
- 1 cup of bananas, mashed
- 1 large egg

Instructions:

1. Set the oven to 370 degrees Fahrenheit. Prepare the muffin baking tray by greasing it or lining it with paper liners.

2. Combine the baking powder, flour, baking soda, and salt in a medium bowl.

3. Combine the banana, sugar, egg, and vanilla extract in another bowl. Blend everything thoroughly. Add applesauce. Add the dry ingredients gradually to the banana mixture. Stir well.

4. Put a scoop of batter into each muffin tin. Bake the muffins for 15-20 minutes, or until a wooden skewer in the middle of one comes out clean. Before serving, allow it to cool down.

Nutritional Info:

Calories: 78 kcal Fat: 0.9 g Protein: 2 g Carbs: 17 g Sugar: 26 g Sodium: 204 mg

15. Egg Salad

Prep Time: 10 minutes

Cook Time: 10 minutes

Servings: 3

Ingredients:

- 1 tbsp. of yellow mustard
- 1/2 cup of mayonnaise
- 1/4 tsp. paprika

- 1/4 cup chopped green onions
- 8 eggs
- A pinch of salt and pepper

Instructions:

1. In a saucepan, add the eggs and then the cold water. Once the water has reached a rolling boil, turn off the heat. Cover the eggs for 10 to 12 minutes and let them sit in hot water. Peel, chop and let cool after removing from boiling water.

2. In a bowl, combine the diced eggs with the mustard, mayonnaise, and green onion. Add paprika, salt, and pepper for seasoning. Serve with any preferred bread or crackers after stirring.

Nutritional Info:

Calories: 180 kcal Fat: 12 g Protein: 14 g Carbs: 3 g Sugar: 2 g Sodium: 325 mg

16. Tuna and Spinach Pancakes

Prep Time: 15 minutes

Cook Time: 10 minutes

Servings: 2

Ingredients:

- 1 teaspoon rapeseed oil
- 2 teaspoons balsamic vinegar(chopped)
- 1 tablespoon tomato puree
- 4 tablespoons plain whole-wheat flour
- 85g cherry tomatoes (chopped)
- 120g can of drained tuna steak
- 200 g of a can of sweetcorn
- 200 g of cottage cheese
- 250 grams of young spinach

- 1 small red onion
- 2 large eggs
- 2 sliced garlic cloves
- 4 pitted Kalamata olives(chopped)
- 10 basil leaves (chopped)

Instructions:

1. Combine all the salad ingredients, then set them aside. In a sizable nonstick pan with hot oil, briefly sauté the garlic. To wilt the spinach, stir in the tomato purée before adding the tuna and cottage cheese. Place aside.

2. Combine the eggs, flour, and 2 tablespoons of water. Heat the remaining oil in a medium nonstick pan, add half the batter, and swirl the pan to coat the bottom. Fry for a few seconds until set, then use a palette knife to flip over and cook the opposite side for one minute. Continue by using the remaining batter. Serve the pancakes with the salad by placing them on serving plates, spreading the filling along one side, and rolling them up.

Nutritional Info:

Calories: 539 kcal Fat: 19 g Protein: 38 g Carbs: 48 g Sugar: 15 g Sodium: 1.5 g

17. Baked Eggs with Greens and Beans

Prep Time: 10 minutes

Cook Time: 20 minutes

Servings: 4

Ingredients:

- 2 teaspoons of mixed herbs
- 2 tablespoons of olive oil, half
- 1 pound of sweet or spicy Italian sausage (optional)
- 1 can of crushed tomatoes
- 1 can of chickpeas

- 1 finely sliced medium yellow onion
- 2 garlic cloves
- ½ cup of Pecorino or Parmesan cheese grated (optional)
- 4 cups stemmed greens
- 6 large eggs
- Salt to taste
- Roasted pepper to taste

Instructions:

1. At 375 degrees, preheat the oven. In an oven-safe skillet, heat the olive oil over medium heat. If using, add the sausage to the pan and cook, breaking it into 1-inch pieces by pushing with the back of a spatula or wooden spoon, for about 8 minutes, until crisp and well cooked. Put aside after being removed using a slotted spoon.

2. Add the onion to the skillet and simmer for 3 to 5 minutes or until tender. Cook the garlic for about a minute until it begins to smell fragrant, then add the chickpeas. Use salt to season. Stir in the tomatoes and sausage after adding them back to the pan. Add the chopped greens to the simmering mixture by handfuls and stir until they are wilted. Use salt to season.

3. Create small holes in the sauce with a spoon, crack the eggs into each one carefully, and season with salt and pepper. Cook in the oven for 7 to 9 minutes or until the eggs are set. Add a tablespoon of grated cheese, if using, and a few herbs over the top.

Nutritional Info:

Calories: 229 kcal Fat: 10 g Protein: 13 g Carbs: 7 g Sugar: 5 g Sodium: 720 mg

18. Apple Cinnamon Porridge

Prep Time: 2 minutes

Cook Time: 5 minutes

Servings: 1

Ingredients:

- 1/2 tsp. of ground cinnamon
- 1 apple
- 30g of oatmeal
- 210ml of semi-skimmed milk

Instructions:

1. While constantly stirring, boil the milk and oats in a saucepan.
2. Simmer for three to five minutes on low heat.
3. No need to peel the apple before adding it; just grate it in. Stir and serve with cinnamon.

Nutritional Info:

Calories: 259 kcal Fat: 5.4 g Protein: 12 g Carbs: 21 g Sugar: 33 g Sodium: 29 mg

19. Strawberry Avocado Smoothie

Prep Time: 5 minutes

Cook Time: 0 minutes

Servings: 2

Ingredients:

- 1 tsp. of flaxseeds
- 1 cup of ice
- 1 cup fresh or frozen strawberries
- 1 cup of avocado
- 1 cup of water
- 2 cups of plain almond milk without sugar
- 1 giant banana
- 1 scoop of protein powder in vanilla

Instructions:

1. All ingredients should be added to a powerful blender. Blend alternating for two to three minutes at low and high speeds to achieve a smooth consistency.
2. Pour into a glass or Mason jar of one's preference and enjoy!

Nutritional Info:

Calories: 315 kcal Fat: 18 g Protein: 14 g Carbs: 31 g Sugar: 12 g Sodium: 386 mg

20. Green Vegetable Fritters

Prep Time: 5 minutes

Cook Time: 20 minutes

Servings: 12

Ingredients:

- 1 tsp. of dill sprigs
- ½ cup of oil
- 1 ½ cups of leftover cooked greens
- A half-clove of garlic
- 1 lemon
- 3 big eggs
- 50 g of cheese remaining
- 250 g of sautéed Brussels sprouts

Instructions:

1. Shred the cooked sprouts and greens that were left behind. Grate the lemon zest finely and peel and slice the garlic. Pick the dill and mince it.

2. Place the shredded greens and sprouts in a basin. Add the cheese crumbles together with the lemon zest, dill, and garlic. After mixing well, add a generous amount of sea salt and black pepper.

3. Add the cracked eggs and stir to combine.

4. Over medium heat, pour a sufficient amount of oil into a big frying pan. When the oil is hot, gently drop a heaping spoonful of the mixture into it and flatten them into tiny patties.

5. When the egg starts to set, fry for 2 to 3 minutes, carefully flip it over, and fry for an additional 2 minutes or until the egg is thoroughly done.

6. Lemons should be cut in half and served on the side for squeezing.

Nutritional Info:

Calories: 32 kcal Fat: 59 g Protein: 3.9 g Carbs: 1 g Sugar: 0.6 g Sodium: 0.3 g

21. Apple Cheese Strudel

Prep Time: 25 minutes

Cook Time: 1 hour

Servings: 1

Ingredients:

- 2 teaspoons of ground cinnamon
- 1 1/2 teaspoon. vanilla extract
- 2 tablespoons. lemon juice
- 2 tablespoons of roasted walnuts
- 2 tablespoons of all-purpose flour
- 6 tablespoons of granulated sugar
- 4 ounces of cream cheese
- 10 ounces of cottage cheese
- 1/2 cup of granulated sugar
- 1/3 cup of regular dry bread crumbs

- 4 apples
- 12 sheets of frozen phyllo dough

Instructions:

2. Prepare a sieve by lining it with a cheesecloth or a coffee filter. Position over the top of a bowl. Cottage cheese should be stuffed inside and then allowed to drain for 15 to 20 minutes.

3. Put the cottage cheese, cream cheese, half a cup of the granulated sugar, and vanilla essence into a food processor and pulse until everything is combined. Run the processor for thirty seconds or until the mixture is smooth. Set aside.

4. While everything is going on, combine the apples, 3 tablespoons of the remaining granulated sugar, the lemon juice, the flour, the walnuts, and the cinnamon in a large basin. Mix well. Toss in order to coat.

5. Set the oven temperature to 400 degrees Fahrenheit. Apply a coating of butter-flavored nonstick spray all over a baking sheet. Bread crumbs and two tablespoons of the remaining granulated sugar should be mixed together in a smaller bowl.

6. Arrange one sheet of phyllo dough on the surface of the work surface with the narrow end facing the cook's direction. Spray a light coating of nonstick coating. Lightly dust with a very little amount (about two scant teaspoons) of the bread-crumb mixture. Repeat the layering process with five of the remaining phyllo sheets, spraying the remaining bread-crumb mixture with nonstick spray and layering with bread crumbs.

7. Cover the bottom layer with half of the cheese filling and spread evenly, leaving a 1-inch border around the edges. Spread one-half of the apple slices across the top in an equal layer. Beginning at the bottom, roll the dough over the filling twice before proceeding to the next step. Continue rolling the object into a cylinder while tucking the sides in.

8. Position, seam-side down, on one end of the baking sheet that has been prepared. To make another strudel, simply repeat the process with the remaining ingredients. Move the ingredients to a baking sheet. Spray each strudel with a nonstick cooking spray and then sprinkle with the remaining 1 tablespoon of sugar.

9. Bake for 15 minutes. Bring the temperature down to 350 degrees F. Bake for 25 to 30 minutes or until the topping is crisp and golden brown. Place on a cooling rack and wait 15 minutes before serving. Serve while still warm or allow to totally cool.

10. To finish the preparation, dust the confectioners' sugar over the strudels. Cut each strudel into 6 diagonal pieces.

Nutritional Info:

Calories: 233 kcal Fat: 15 g Protein: 3 g Carbs: 26 g Sugar: 13 g Sodium: 62 mg

22. Vegetable Breakfast Bakes

Prep Time: 15 minutes

Cook Time: 30 minutes

Servings: 4

Ingredients:

- 2 tsp olive oil
- 1 clove of garlic
- 4 eggs
- 4 huge mushrooms
- 8 tomatoes
- 200g bag spinach

Instructions:

1. Preheat oven to 200 degrees Celsius (180 degrees Celsius with the fan on) 6. Distribute the tomatoes and mushrooms among the four oven-safe dishes. After dividing the garlic among the dishes, drizzle oil on top, sprinkle some spice on top, and then place in the oven for ten minutes.

2. In the meantime, place the spinach in a large colander and pour a kettle of boiling water over it. This will wilt the spinach. First, remove any extra water from the spinach and stir it into the meals. Create a little space between the vegetables, and then break an egg into each dish. Place back in the oven and continue to cook for an additional 8 to 10 minutes or until the egg has reached the desired doneness.

Nutritional Info:

Calories: 127 kcal Fat: 8 g Protein: 9 g Carbs: 5 g Sugar: 5 g Sodium: 10 mg

23. Fat Burning Smoothie

Prep Time: 2 minutes

Cook Time: 3 minutes

Servings: 1

Ingredients:

- 2 tablespoons of fresh mint
- 1 stalk of chopped celery
- ½ cup of iced green tea
- ½ of an avocado
- ½ cup grapefruit
- 1 cup of chopped spinach
- 1 cup of frozen pineapple

Instructions:

1. Put spinach, mint, celery, and green tea in a blender. Blend until smooth.
2. Blend to a silky smoothness.

3. Mix in the ingredients that are left over.

4. Combine once more. When served cold, smoothies taste the best.

Nutritional Info:

Calories: 231 kcal Fat: 8 g Protein: 4 g Carbs: 42 g Sugar: 26 g Sodium: 35 mg

24. Chia Pudding

Prep Time: 10 minutes

Cook Time: 1 hour

Servings: 1

Ingredients:

- ½ tablespoon of maple syrup
- 1/4 a teaspoon of vanilla extract
- 4 teaspoons worth of chia seeds
- 1 cup almond milk
- A handful of fresh berries or other types of fruit

Instructions:

1. Combine the chia seeds, maple syrup, milk, and vanilla extract, if using, in a bowl or mason jar

and whisk until smooth. In order to thoroughly combine the ingredients, simply cover the jar if using with its lid, and give it a good shake.

2. After all of the ingredients for the chia pudding have been thoroughly combined, let the mixture sit for five minutes, then give it another toss to breakdown any clumps of chia seeds, cover it, and place it in the fridge to set for one to two hours or overnight. It is important that the chia pudding be lovely and thick rather than runny. If one finds that it is not thick enough, simply add a little bit more chia seed (about 1 tablespoon), give it a swirl, and place it back in the refrigerator for another half an hour or so.

3. Chia pudding can be kept fresh in the refrigerator for up to five to seven days if it is sealed tightly in an airtight container.

Nutritional Info:

Calories: 170 kcal Fat: 7 g Protein: 9 g Carbs: 16 g Sugar: 3 g Sodium: 90 mg

25. Cranberry and Raspberry Smoothie

Prep Time: 10 minutes

Cook Time: 0 minutes

Servings: 4

Ingredients:

- 1 tablespoon of caster sugar

- 100ml of milk.
- 200ml natural yogurt
- 400 ml of cranberry juice
- 2 cups of frozen raspberry

Instructions:

1. Put all of the materials into a mixer and whir them around until they're completely smooth. Pour into glasses, then garnish with mint, and serve immediately.

Nutritional Info:

Calories: 100 kcal Fat: 2 g Protein: 4 g Carbs: 17 g Sugar: 17 g Sodium: 10 mg

Chapter 4: Vegetable Recipes

26. Mushroom Alfredo Cauliflower Gnocchi

Prep Time: 5 minutes

Cook Time: 15 minutes

Servings: 2

Ingredients:

- 2 tbsp. of olive oil
- 1 cup of sliced mushrooms
- 2 cups of baby spinach
- 1 packet of cauliflower gnocchi
- 1 jar of mushroom sauce/alfredo sauce

Instructions:

1. To heat the olive oil, place it in a skillet of around medium size and set it over medium heat. Add the frozen cauliflower gnocchi and the cut mushrooms after the mixture are warm enough to start shimmering. Sauté for 6 to 8 minutes, or until cauliflower gnocchi is heated through and starts to crisp up on the outside and mushrooms have softened and turned to brown.

2. Bring the Alfredo gnocchi to a gentle simmer after stirring in the Mushroom Mixture Alfredo Sauce. Serve warm after adding spinach and cooking it thoroughly.

Nutritional Info:

Calories: 745 kcal Fat: 34 g Protein: 21 g Carbs: 100 g Sugar: 8 g Sodium: 2651 mg

27. Cauliflower Pizza Crust

Prep Time: 15 minutes

Cook Time: 1 hour 10 minutes

Servings: 4

Ingredients:

- 1/2 teaspoon of garlic powder
- 1/2 tsp. oregano
- 1/8 teaspoon of onion powder
- 1/tsp. salt
- 1 tbsp. of fresh parmesan
- 1/2 cup of new arugula

- 1 cup of tomato pesto
- 1 cup of mushrooms in sauce
- 1 cup cream cheese
- 6 cups of cauliflower florets
- 1 beaten egg
- 1 big fresh mozzarella ball
- 5–6 large black olives

Instructions:

1. Cook cauliflower florets until they can be broken up with a fork in a big pot of boiling water. 12 min. Approximately. Drain thoroughly and let cool. Ring out the juice from the cauliflower using a nut bag. It should produce roughly 1.5 cups of liquid. The more moisture one can extract from the cauliflower, the crispier the crust will be.
2. Set the oven to 425 °F.
3. Combine the cooked cauliflower, salt, cream cheese, onion powder, garlic powder, and oregano in a sizable bowl. With a fork, shred the cauliflower, then combine it with the cheese, eggs, and spices.
4. With hands, flatten the cauliflower mixture into a circle about 1/4" thick circle and place it on a pizza stone or baking sheet lined with parchment paper.
5. 30 minutes of baking are required; place on the middle oven rack. After taking the pizza out of the oven, cover the top with fresh parchment paper. Flip the pizza crust with care so that the top is now facing down. At this point, the parchment won't stick to anything anymore, so one can remove it altogether if one chooses. Cook for a further 15 minutes or until the edges are crispy and brown.
6. Take the baked pizza crust out of the oven and add any preferred toppings. The recipe is topped with mozzarella cheese, mushrooms, and olives after spreading tomato pesto on it. Cook for an additional 5-8 minutes or until the cheese is melted. Take out of the oven, let cool for five minutes, then top with arugula and cut.

Nutritional Info:

Calories: 462 kcal Fat: 39 g Protein: 25 g Carbs: 16 g Sugar: 5 g Sodium: 1363 mg

28. Mushroom Risotto

Prep Time: 10 minutes

Cook Time: 45 minutes

Servings: 6

Ingredients:

- 1/8 teaspoon each of salt and freshly ground pepper
- 1-tbsp. lemon juice
- 1 tbsp. minced fresh parsley
- 8 tbsp. of butter
- 3/4 cup of dry white wine
- 1 cup of heavy cream
- 1 cup of freshly grated parmesan cheese
- 1 1/2 cups Rice
- 2 cups of mushrooms
- 5 cups of chicken stock (or vegetable)
- 2 minced tiny shallots
- 2 new thyme sprigs
- 4 minced garlic cloves

Instructions:

1. In a little saucepan, warm the broth slowly.
2. Melt half of the butter in a large skillet over medium heat. Add the shallots and mushrooms, and cook for 8 minutes or until they are soft. Stir in the garlic, thyme sprigs, salt, and pepper for one more minute. Take the mushroom mixture out of the pan and set it aside.
3. Over medium heat, add the remaining butter to the pan. Once melted, add the rice and stir for 3–4 minutes or until the rice turns translucent.
4. Add 1/4 cup of dry white wine and the lemon juice, then cook while stirring continuously until

the liquid is absorbed. Stir in either 1 cup of vegetable broth or mushroom stock until almost all of the broth has been absorbed. Continue adding broth, 1 cup at a time, while stirring, and do so until the liquid is nearly absorbed. This process requires 20 to 25 minutes.

5. Stir the rice and the mushroom mixture together. Add heavy cream and parmesan cheese gently, then simmer over low heat for an additional 5 minutes. The texture of risotto must be creamy but firm. Add freshly ground pepper, parmesan cheese shavings, and fresh parsley to the risotto before placing it in a serving bowl.

Nutritional Info:

Calories: 450 kcal Fat: 20 g Protein: 14 g Carbs: 49 g Sugar: 5 g Sodium: 297 mg

29. Vegetable Lasagna

Prep Time: 15 minutes

Cook Time: 3 hours

Servings: 7

Ingredients:

- 1/2 tsp. of ground pepper
- 1 tsp garlic powder
- 1 tsp salt

- 2 tbsp. of thinly sliced parmesan
- 8 ounces of mushrooms
- 15 ounces of ricotta cheese
- 16 ounces of grates mozzarella
- 15 oz. of ricotta cheese,
- 2 small yellow squash (sliced)
- 2 big eggs
- 2 cups spinach
- 2 small zucchini
- 1/3 cup of minced basil
- 250 ml jar of pasta sauce
- A 1-pound box of lasagna noodles

Instructions:

1. Combine the eggs, salt, pepper, garlic powder, ricotta, and basil in a medium bowl.
2. Spread 1/4 cup of pasta sauce in the bottom of a 5-quart slow cooker, then arrange uncooked lasagna noodles on top. Then, distribute 1/3 of the ricotta mixture.
3. Three-quarters of each type of vegetable (mushroom, zucchini, and yellow squash) should then be layered on top, followed by one-third of each of the chopped spinach and shredded mozzarella. Add the last layer, 1/4 of the sauce.
4. Repeat the entire procedure two more times, beginning with the dried lasagna. Add a layer of dried pasta, the last of the sauce, and a layer of fresh mozzarella to finish.
5. Place a clean dish towel between the lid and the slow cooker to catch any extra liquid created by the crock pot's steam.
6. Cook the noodles on high heat for three hours or until they are soft and the sauce has been absorbed.
7. Add some additional basil and freshly grated parmesan cheese to finish.

Nutritional Info:

Calories: 690 kcal Fat: 29 g Protein: 42 g Carbs: 69 g Sugar: 10 g Sodium: 1072 mg

30. Stuffed Peppers

Prep Time: 20 minutes

Cook Time: 1 hour 20 minutes

Servings: 6

Ingredients:

- 1 teaspoon of salt
- 1 tablespoon vegetable oil or extra virgin olive oil
- 1 tablespoon fresh cilantro minced (optional)
- 2 tablespoons of taco seasoning
- 1 cup of corn, frozen
- 1 cup of pepper jack cheese, shredded
- 1 cup raw rice, white
- 1 2/3 cups vegetable stock
- 1 can drain black beans
- 1 can tomato dice
- 1/2 medium-sized yellow onion, chopped
- 3 to 4 chopped green onions
- 4 large red peppers

Instructions:

1. Place a rack in the middle of the oven and preheat to 400°F. Use olive oil to grease a baking dish.
2. Trim, remove the seeds from, and dice one of the bell peppers. The remaining bell peppers should be cut in half lengthwise while attempting to preserve as much of the stems as possible. Throw out the ribs and seeds.

3. In a big skillet over medium heat, warm the oil. When the oil is shimmering, add the onion and cook, stirring, for about 4 minutes or until slightly softened. Add the salt and rice, then simmer for an additional three minutes. Add the bell pepper, tomatoes, green onions, taco spice, and broth and mix well. To boil, add the rice mixture. Lower the heat, cover, and simmer for about 25 minutes or until the rice is tender. Corn and black beans should be thoroughly mixed and heated before being added.

4. Place the peppers on the baking dish that has been prepared, then equally distribute the rice mixture inside each one. Put cheese on top. For about 40 minutes, bake the cheese uncovered until it bubbles and turns golden.

5. If wanted, top with cilantro and serve.

Nutritional Info:

Calories: 319 kcal Fat: 9 g Protein: 12 g Carbs: 49 g Sugar: 10 g Sodium: 626 mg

31. Pan Quesadilla with Jalapeno Ranch

Prep Time: 20 minutes

Cook Time: 25 minutes

Servings: 6

Ingredients:

- 1/2 teaspoon of salt
- 1 teaspoon of garlic powder

- 1 teaspoon onion powder
- 2 tablespoons of lime juice
- 1/2 cup of mayonnaise
- 1/2 cup soured cream
- ½ cup of pickles
- 1/2 cup minced green onions
- 1/4 cup finely minced cilantro
- 1 cup pepper jack cheese
- 1 cup grated mozzarella
- 2 big avocados, sliced thin
- 10 flour tortillas

Instructions:

1. Set the oven to 425 °F.
2. Place six tortillas around the edge of a sizable baking sheet that has been buttered, with half of each tortilla dangling over the side. Add two more tortillas to the baking sheet's center.
3. Then add sliced avocados, green onions, and shredded cheese on top.
4. Finish by placing two additional tortillas on top of the filling and folding the extra tortilla into the center to cover it. To keep tortillas flat while baking, liberally brushes or spray them with oil before setting them on top of a second baking sheet that has been previously coated. Bake till brown and crispy for 20 minutes with the cover on, then for 5 minutes without.
5. One may make the jalapeno ranch by combining all the ingredients in a food processor, blender, or immersion blender while the quesadilla is cooking.
6. Serve quesadillas dipped in jalapeno ranch after cutting them into big squares.

Nutritional Info:

Calories: 543 kcal Fat: 34 g Protein: 13 g Carbs: 48 g Sugar: 4 g Sodium: 1375 mg

32. Vegetarian Chili

Prep Time: 15 minutes

Cook Time: 1 hour 15 minutes

Servings: 10

Ingredients:

- 2 teaspoons of salt
- 2 teaspoons cumin
- 1 tablespoon cilantro
- 1 tablespoon green onions
- 2 tablespoon avocado
- 2 tablespoons of olive oil
- 1 chopped large yellow onion
- 1 chopped red bell pepper
- 1 chopped green bell pepper
- 2 chopped sweet potatoes
- 4 chopped garlic cloves

- 1 can of black beans
- 1 can of pinto beans
- 1 can of kidney beans
- 1 can tomatoes
- 1 can red enchilada sauce
- 1 bay leaf
- 30 grams of chili powder

Instructions:

1. In a sizable Dutch oven or soup pot, heat the oil. Saute sweet potatoes, bell peppers, and onions for about 4-5 minutes or until the onions start to soften. Add the garlic after the first two minutes of sautéing.
2. After adding the beans and tomatoes, stir in the salt, cumin, chili powder, bay leaves, and enchilada sauce. Just enough water should be added to cover the beans. (Roughly 1–2 cups.)
3. Bring the water to a boil. Simmer with the lid off for one hour, frequently stirring to ensure nothing clings to the bottom.
4. Serve garnished with avocado, cilantro, and green onions.

Nutritional Info:

Calories: 228 kcal Fat: 5 g Protein: 10 g Carbs: 38 g Sugar: 8 g Sodium: 830 mg

33. Stir Fry Tofu with Peanut Sauce

Prep Time: 15 minutes

Cook Time: 20 minutes

Servings: 4

Ingredients:

- 1 teaspoon siracha
- 1 tablespoon grated or chopped fresh ginger
- 1 tablespoon sesame seeds (optional)
- 2 tablespoons of canola oil
- 2 tablespoons of roasted sesame oil
- 3 tablespoons of apple cider vinegar
- 1/2 cup organic peanut butter (unsalted)
- 1/4 cup of soy sauce reduced in salt (or tamari)
- 1/4 cup of water
- 2 cups of cabbage (chopped)
- 1 (14 oz.) cut into 1-inch cube tofu

- 1 small head of broccoli, separated into florets
- 1-batch peanut sauce
- 1 big clove of minced garlic
- A handful of thinly sliced green onions

Instructions:

1. In a blender or food processor, combine all the ingredients for the peanut sauce. Process or blend for about 30 seconds or until the mixture is creamy, cohesive, and smooth. Simple to prepare a few days ahead of time and keep in the refrigerator.

2. Warm the oil in a sizable skillet or wok over medium-high heat. Add the tofu and cook it for 10–12 minutes altogether, a few minutes on each side. Remove the tofu from the skillet once it has become crispy and place it on a plate covered with paper towels.

3. Add the cabbage and broccoli to the same skillet and cook for about 8 minutes or until the vegetables are soft and tender. Return the tofu to the skillet and reduce the heat to medium-low before stirring in the peanut sauce. Allow simmering for a further 1-2 minutes after tossing to coat.

4. Serve plain or with steamed brown rice or noodles.

Nutritional Info:

Calories: 540 kcal Fat: 35 g Protein: 21 g Carbs: 19 g Sugar: 4 g Sodium: 845 mg

34. Vegetarian Meatballs

Prep Time: 25 minutes

Cook Time: 45 minutes

Servings: 6

Ingredients:

- 1/4 teaspoon cayenne
- 2 1/2 teaspoons of salt (divided)
- 3 teaspoons of Italian seasoning (divided)
- 1/2 cup olive oil

- 1/4 cup of olive oil
- 1 cup of parmesan cheese
- 1 1/2 cups panko breadcrumbs
- 2 1/2 cups cooked lentils
- 1 cooked Pasta
- 1 small onion chopped
- 2 eggs
- 8 ounces of mushrooms
- 3 minced garlic cloves
- 2 pounds of tomatoes
- Handful of Basil

Instructions:

1. Set the oven to 400 °F. Combine tomato halves with 1/4 cup of extra virgin olive oil, 1 teaspoon of Italian spice, and 1 teaspoon of salt in a large bowl. Place the cut-side-up tomatoes in a single layer on a large baking sheet and set aside.

2. Put dried lentils in a small pot and bring them up to medium-high. Water should be poured over them to a depth of about 4 inches. They should be brought to a boil, then reduced to a simmer for about 20 minutes, uncovered until they are soft but not mushy. Remove any extra water, then set it aside.

3. The mushrooms should be processed in a food processor until they resemble peas in size.

4. In a large pan over medium-high heat, warm 1 tablespoon of oil. Add the onion to the hot oil and cook for three minutes or until transparent. After the liquid has evaporated and the garlic is fragrant, add the garlic and the mushrooms that have been pulsed. Sauté for a further 3–4 minutes.

5. After turning off the heat, add the lentils and the skillet's contents back to the blender. About 20 pulses, scraping down in the middle until mixed.

6. Combine the mushroom lentil mixture with the panko bread crumbs, eggs, parmesan cheese, cayenne, 2 teaspoons of Italian spice, and 1 12 teaspoon of salt in a large bowl. Stir to combine.

7. 1 1/2 tablespoon-sized balls of the mixture, formed by rolling it, should be placed on a different baking sheet.
8. Give the meatballs a light coating of cooking spray or 1 tablespoon of olive oil.
9. Turning the two baking sheets and flip the meatballs after 15 minutes of baking the tomatoes and meatballs.
10. Toss the cooked spaghetti, 14 cups of olive oil, fresh basil, and freshly grated parmesan cheese with the roasted tomatoes and meatballs.

Nutritional Info:

Calories: 514 kcal Fat: 30g Protein: 39 g Carbs: 30 g Sugar: 3 g Sodium: 1677 mg

35. Tofu Lettuce Wraps

Prep Time: 10 minutes

Cook Time: 15 minutes

Servings: 6

Ingredients:

- 1 teaspoon lime zest
- 1 teaspoon of chili paste
- 2 teaspoon salt
- 2 teaspoons of brown sugar
- 1 tablespoon lime juice
- 1 tablespoon sesame oil
- 1-tablespoon brown sugar
- 2 tablespoons of chili paste
- 2 tablespoons soy sauce
- 1/2 cup of roasted grain white rice (optional)
- 1/2 cup coarsely chopped fresh cilantro
- 1/2 cup finely sliced shallots

- 1/2 cup roughly chopped peanuts (optional)
- 1/3 cup of lime juice
- 1/4 cup fresh mint leaves
- 1 pound of firm tofu (crushed)
- 2 heads of lettuce
- 3-5 green onions (sliced)

Instructions:

1. In a little sauté pan, lightly brown and fragrantly toast the raw, oil-free sushi rice. Use a food processor or a high-speed blender to grind the toasted rice into a fine powder. Place aside.
2. Over medium heat, cook the shallots in the oil in a big skillet for 3 minutes.
3. Add the tofu crumbles and cook for 5 minutes or until heated through.
4. Add the brown sugar, chili paste, lime juice, zest, and powdered, toasted rice (if using). Until all the ingredients are well-combined, sauté for 3 to 5 minutes. Get rid of the heat. If the rice isn't entirely cooked, let the tofu filling sit for 5 minutes to soften the rice.
5. All of the components for the tofu lettuce wrap sauce should be combined in a small bowl.
6. Toss the tofu mixture with the peanuts, cilantro, mint, and green onions.
7. Take the lettuce leaves off the stem. With the tofu mixture, stuff each lettuce leaf. If preferred, drizzle with additional fresh herbs and a small amount of sauce. Enjoy!

Nutritional Info:

Calories: 221 kcal Fat: 13 g Protein: 12 g Carbs: 17 g Sugar: 6 g Sodium: 254 mg

36. Creamy Zucchini Pasta

Prep Time: 8 minutes

Cook Time: 20 minutes

Servings: 6

Ingredients:

- 1/2 teaspoon freshly ground black pepper

- 1 teaspoon salt
- 1 tablespoon minced garlic
- 1/2 cup of pasta water
- 1/4 cup of olive oil
- 3/4 cup grated Parmesan cheese
- 1 cup of heavy cream
- 3 cups of shredded zucchini
- 1 lb of long pasta
- 2 thinly sliced tiny shallots
- 20 leaves of basil

Instructions:

1. Warm the olive oil in a medium-sized saucepan over medium heat.
2. Add the shallots and zucchini, and simmer for 8 to 10 minutes or until tender.
3. Cook for another minute after adding the garlic.
4. Add heavy cream, salt, basil leaves, and pepper once the vegetables are very soft. Stirring often, bring to a gentle simmer and cook for 5 minutes.
5. Cook the pasta as directed on the package in salted water while the sauce is simmering. Keep 1/2 cup of the pasta water aside before draining the pasta.
6. Pour pasta water into the zucchini sauce. Before transferring the sauce to a high-speed blender, remove it from the heat and let it cool. Smoothly blend the sauce. Add spaghetti and Parmesan cheese to the sauce after transferring it back to the sauce pan.
7. Serve pasta tossed in sauce, sprinkled with additional parmesan and freshly ground pepper, and more pasta water if it's too thick.

Nutritional Info:

Calories: 555 kcal Fat: 29 g Protein: 15 g Carbs: 63 g Sugar: 4 g Sodium: 212 mg

37. Green Curry Buddha Bowl

Prep Time: 10 minutes

Cook Time: 5 minutes

Servings: 6

Ingredients:

- 1/2 teaspoon salt
- 2 teaspoons olive oil
- 2 teaspoons of fish sauce
- 1–2 teaspoons brown sugar
- 1 tablespoon lime juice
- 2 tablespoons green curry paste
- 1 cup julienned carrots
- 1 cup of raw cashews
- 2 cups of broccoli florets
- 4 cups cooked brown rice

- 1/4 head purple cabbage
- 6-8 large mushrooms (sliced)
- 14 oz. coconut cream can
- A handful of lime wedges
- Handful of cilantro

Instructions:

1. In a blender, combine all the ingredients and blend on high for two minutes to create the curry sauce.
2. Put the mushrooms and olive oil in a small bowl. Over low heat, place a pot with a steaming basket attached and one inch of water inside. Place the broccoli and mushrooms in the steamer basket and steam for 5 minutes or until the broccoli is soft.
3. Layer the vegetables over the brown rice in the bowl, then drizzle with the curry sauce. Sprinkle on some cilantro, toasted coconut, and a squeeze of lime as garnish.

Nutritional Info:

Calories: 398 kcal Fat: 25 g Protein: 9 g Carbs: 35 g Sugar: 4 g Sodium: 488 mg

38. Burrito Bowl with Crema

Prep Time: 20 minutes

Cook Time: 30 minutes

Servings: 6

Ingredients:

- 1/2 teaspoon salt
- 2 tablespoons of lime juice
- 3 tablespoons Citrus juice
- 1/2 cup salsa
- 1/2 cup soured cream
- 1/3 cup of olive oil

- 1/4 cup Cilantro
- 1/4 cup of taco seasoning
- 2 cups of lettuce (chopped)
- 4 cups lime-cilantro rice
- 1 avocado
- 1 minced garlic clove
- 1 ½ red bell pepper
- ½ onion (sliced)
- 1 cauliflower head (separated into florets)
- 1 green bell pepper (thinly sliced)
- 1 can of black beans
- Handful of cilantro

Instructions:

1. Set the oven to 400 degrees Fahrenheit.
2. Spread out the cauliflower, onion, and bell peppers on a large baking sheet after tossing them with the lime juice, taco seasoning, and olive oil in a big bowl.
3. Bake on the center rack for 30 minutes, or until the cauliflower is soft with crispy edges.
4. Prepare avocado crema by combining all the ingredients in a food processor or small blender and churning until smooth while the vegetables are cooking.
5. Combine the beans and salsa in a small skillet over medium heat, and cook for 5 minutes or until heated through.
6. Over cilantro rice, top the roasted taco vegetables with the beans, lettuce, and avocado crema.

Nutritional Info:

Calories: 410 kcal Fat: 21 g Protein: 8 g Carbs: 52 g Sugar: 7 g Sodium: 590 mg

39. Garlic and Seasame Ramen Noodles

Prep Time: 10 minutes

Cook Time: 15 minutes

Servings: 4

Ingredients:

- 1 teaspoon sesame seeds
- 1 teaspoon freshly grated ginger
- 1/2–1 teaspoon of sriracha
- 2 teaspoons of minced garlic
- 1 tablespoon rice vinegar
- 1 tablespoon brown sugar (optional)
- 2 tablespoons toasted sesame oil
- 1/4 cup of soy sauce
- 1/4 cup of water
- 1/4 cup hoisin sauce
- 3 packages of instant ramen
- 4-6 finely sliced green onions

Instructions:

1. Cook the ramen for 3–4 minutes as directed on the package in a large saucepan of boiling water; drain well.
2. Mix the soy sauce, rice vinegar, oyster sauce, brown sugar, chili sauce, and water in a small bowl.
3. In a large skillet over medium heat, warm the sesame oil.
4. Add the ginger and garlic, stirring until fragrant, approximately a minute.
5. Pour the sauce into the pan, then let it simmer for 3–4 minutes. About three minutes later, add the cooked ramen noodles and stir until they are well heated and coated in sauce.

6. Add green onions and sesame seeds as a garnish.

Nutritional Info:

Calories: 402 kcal Fat: 18 g Protein: 10 g Carbs: 49 g Sugar: 5 g Sodium: 1145 mg

40. Cauliflower Taco with Avocado Crema

Prep Time: 15 minutes

Cook Time: 20 minutes

Servings: 4

Ingredients:

- 1/2 teaspoon salt
- 2 tablespoons taco seasoning
- 2 tablespoons of lime juice
- 2 tablespoons of olive oil
- 1/2 cup sour cream
- 1/4 cup cilantro
- 1/4 cup lime juice

- 1 avocado
- 1 minced garlic clove
- 1 large cauliflower head (divided into little florets)
- 1 shredded cabbage

Handful of Cilantro

Instructions:

1. Set the oven to 400 °F.
2. Spread the cauliflower out on a large baking sheet after tossing it with taco spice, olive oil, and lime juice in a big bowl.
3. Bake for 30 minutes, or until cauliflower is cooked with crispy edges, on the center rack.
4. Put all the ingredients for the avocado crema in a food processor or small blender and pulse until smooth while the cauliflower is roasting.
5. Add roasted cauliflower, shredded cabbage, and fresh cilantro to warm tortillas. Add avocado crema over the top before serving.

Nutritional Info:

Calories: 349 kcal Fat: 20 g Protein: 8 g Carbs: 40 g Sugar: 10 g Sodium: 495 mg

Chapter 5: Seafood Recipes

41. Seafood Enchiladas

Prep Time: 15 minutes

Cook Time: 1 hour

Servings: 8

Ingredients:

- 1/4 teaspoon salt
- 1/4 teaspoon freshly ground pepper
- 2 teaspoons of canola oil
- 1/2 cup of green onions (finely sliced)
- 1/2 cup minced onion
- 1/4 cup minced red sweet pepper
- 3/4 cup fat-free milk
- 5 cups of water

- 1 1/4 pounds shrimp
- 1 carton of light sour cream
- 2 fresh chopped poblano chiles
- 2 minced garlic cloves
- 8 low-carb tortillas 4 ounces softened cheese
- 8 ounces of fresh or frozen sea bass

Instructions:

1. Thaw any frozen shrimp and halibut. Devein and peel the shrimp. Rinse the shrimp and halibut, then use paper towels to pat them dry. Bake at 350 degrees Fahrenheit. Prepare a 3-quart rectangle baking dish with cooking spray. Bring the water to a boil in a large saucepan. Add the shrimp; cook, occasionally stirring, for 1 to 3 minutes or until opaque. Drain and chop after a cold water rinse. Set apart.

2. Measure the fish's thickness in step two. In a sizable skillet or 4-quart Dutch oven with a secure lid, put a steamer. Fill the skillet with water until it is just above the steamer insert. Bring the water in the skillet to a boil. In the steamer insert, put the fish. When the fish flakes easily when examined with a fork, cover and steam it over medium heat for 4 to 6 minutes per 1/2-inch thickness, adding extra water as necessary to maintain steam. Set aside after flaking the fish into bite-sized pieces.

3. Heat oil over medium heat in a sizable nonstick skillet. Add the onion, sweet pepper, and chile peppers; simmer, occasionally turning, for 5 to 10 minutes or until the veggies are soft. Add garlic and heat for an additional minute. Eliminate heat. Stir in the halibut and shrimp.

4. Wrap the stack of tortillas in foil securely in the meantime. Bake for approximately 10 minutes or until thoroughly heated. Use an electric mixer to smooth up the cream cheese in a medium bowl for the sauce. Add sour cream, flour, a quarter teaspoon of salt, and some black pepper. Until smooth, gradually beat in milk.

5. Stir thoroughly, and add 1/2 cup of the sauce to the shrimp mixture. Distribute the shrimp mixture among the tortillas, spooning it close to the edge of each tortilla. Wrap tortillas in rolls. Lay the filled tortillas seam-side down in the baking pan that has been prepped. Topping tortillas with the remaining sauce.

6. Bake for about 35 minutes, covered until heated all the way through. 5 minutes should pass before serving. Green onions should be added just before serving.

Nutritional Info:

Calories: 283 kcal Fat:11 g Protein: 23 g Carbs: 21 g Sugar: 2 g Sodium: 540 mg

42. Shrimp and Corn Succotash

Prep Time: 15 minutes

Cook Time: 10 minutes

Servings: 4

Ingredients:

- 1 teaspoon Cajun seasoning
- 1/2 teaspoon ground black pepper
- 1/2 teaspoon salt
- 1/2 cup of onions (chopped)
- 1/4 cup fresh basil (chopped)
- 2/3 cup red bell pepper (chopped)
- 1 1/2 cups of frozen lima beans
- 1 1/2 cups fresh kernels of corn
- 2 1/2 cups of olive oil
- 1-pound deveined shrimp

Instructions:

1. Combine lima beans with 1/2 cup water in a medium microwave-safe bowl. Microwave for 5 minutes on high, covered. Drain and expose.
2. In the meantime, combine the shrimp with the Cajun spice in a big dish. Over medium-high heat, preheat a large skillet. Swirl in 1 tablespoon of oil to coat the pan. Add the shrimp to the pan and cook them for three minutes, occasionally flipping them. Take the shrimp out of the pan and cover them to keep them warm.

3. Stir in the remaining 1 1/2 tablespoons of oil to coat the pan. Saute the bell pepper and onion for about 6 minutes or until they are almost soft. Add the corn and cook for 2 minutes or until crisp-tender. Add the lima beans along with the salt and pepper. Once the heat is off, whisk in the basil. Add shrimp on top.

Nutritional Info:

Calories: 358 kcal Fat: 11 g Protein: 30 g Carbs: 33 g Sugar: 10 g Sodium: 318 mg

43. Rosemary Salmon with Potatoes and Asparagus

Prep Time: 20 minutes

Cook Time: 30 minutes

Servings: 4

Ingredients:

- 1/2 teaspoon whole-grain mustard
- 1 teaspoon of salt
- 1 teaspoon of ground pepper
- 3 teaspoons olive oil
- 2 teaspoons of garlic (chopped)

- 1 tablespoon balsamic glaze
- 1 tablespoon rosemary (chopped)
- 1 pound of asparagus (chopped)
- 1 ¼ pound Yukon Gold potatoes (chopped)
- 1 small lemon
- 4 skinless salmon fillets

Instructions:

1. Set oven to 425 degrees Fahrenheit.
2. In a small bowl, combine oil, rosemary, and garlic. Put the potatoes in a large bowl and season with salt and pepper and 1 tablespoon of the oil mixture. Place the potatoes on a large baking sheet with a rim in an equal layer. Roast for about 20 minutes or until soft and gently browned. To one end of the pan, push the potatoes.
3. With 1 tablespoon of the oil combination, 1/4 teaspoon salt, and 1/8 teaspoon pepper, add the asparagus to the big bowl and toss to combine. On the other end of the baking sheet, arrange the asparagus. It takes around 3 minutes to roast asparagus to a bright green color. Push the vegetables to the pan's edges to make room in the center.
4. The additional 1/4 teaspoon salt and 1/8 teaspoon pepper should be added after brushing the salmon with the remaining 1 tablespoon of the oil mixture. In the middle of the pan, place the salmon. Slice the lemon in half, then arrange the segments around the fish and vegetables. Five more minutes of roasting. The remaining lemon half should be cut into wedges.
5. In a small bowl, combine the mustard and balsamic glaze. Apply the salmon with 1 tablespoon of the mixture. Continue roasting for a further 5 minutes or until the veggies are soft and the salmon is barely cooked through. Pour the remaining sauce over the vegetables. With the lemon wedges, serve.

Nutritional Info:

Calories: 400 kcal Fat: 15 g Protein: 32 g Carbs: 34 g Sugar: 6 g Sodium: 711 mg

44. Shrimp and Cauliflower Bake

Prep Time: 40 minutes

Cook Time: 20 minutes

Servings: 4

Ingredients:

- 1 teaspoon lemon zest
- ½ teaspoon of red pepper flakes
- 1/4 teaspoon of salt
- 1 tables poon of freshly chopped dill
- 2 tablespoons of olive oil
- 1/2 cup onions (chopped)
- ½ cup crumbled feta cheese
- 4 cups of cauliflower florets
- 1 pound of medium shrimp
- 2 cans of diced tomatoes
- 2 minced garlic cloves
- 4 slices of lemon

Instructions:

1. Set oven to 425 degrees Fahrenheit. Combine the cauliflower, onion, oil, salt, and crushed red pepper in a large bowl. In a small, shallow metal roasting pan, spread the ingredients out. Bake the cauliflower for 25 minutes or just until it's soft.

2. Meanwhile, rinse and pat dry the shrimp. Combine shrimp, tomatoes, garlic, and lemon zest in a medium bowl. Over the cauliflower mixture, pour the shrimp mixture. Bake the shrimp for a further 15 minutes or until opaque.

3. Cheese and dill combined, then sprinkled over shrimp mixture. Serve with lemon slices, if desired.

Nutritional Info:

Calories: 269 kcal Fat: 10.9 g Protein: 29 g Carbs: 18 g Sugar: 9.5 g Sodium: 561 mg

45. Fish and Shrimp Stew

Prep Time: 5 minutes

Cook Time: 30 minutes

Servings: 4

Ingredients:

- 1/2 teaspoon garlic
- 1/4 teaspoon of salt
- 1/8 teaspoon of ground black pepper
- 1 teaspoon dried oregano
- 1 tablespoon parsley
- 2 teaspoons of virgin olive oil
- 2 cut celery stalks
- 6 ounces of shrimp

- 8 ounces of skinless fish fillets
- 1/3 cup minced onion
- 1/4 cup dry white wine
- 1 cup of chicken broth
- 1 can of diced tomatoes
- 1 can of tomato sauce

Instructions:

1. Into 1-1/2-inch slices, cut the fish. Shrimp should be cut lengthwise in half. Keep chilled until it's ready to use.

2. Oil is heated in a big pot over medium heat. For about 5 minutes, while tossing regularly, sauté the onion, celery, and garlic until they are soft. Stir in 1 cup of the broth and the wine slowly up to a boil. Cook for 5 minutes at a simmer after lowering the heat. Add the tomato sauce, oregano, salt, and pepper along with the drained tomatoes. Once again, at a boil, lower the heat to a simmer, cover the pan, and cook for 5 minutes.

3. Add shrimp and fish, stirring gently. Bring back to a boil, then immediately turn down the heat. Shrimp should be opaque, and the fish should flake readily with a fork after 3 to 5 minutes of simmering. Parsley should be added just before serving.

Nutritional Info:

Calories: 165 kcal Fat: 4 g Protein: 19 g Carbs: 13 g Sugar: 26 g Sodium: 449 mg

46. Panko and Parmesan Crusted Scallops

Prep Time: 10 minutes

Cook Time: 20 minutes

Servings: 4

Ingredients:

- 1/4 teaspoon salt
- 1/4 teaspoon of pepper, ground
- 2 teaspoons parsley
- 2 tablespoons of lemon juice
- 2 tablespoons of shallot (chopped)
- 2 tablespoons of butter
- 3 tablespoons of olive oil
- 1 pound of big seas shallots
- 1/2 cup of whole wheat panko breadcrumbs
- 1/4 cup Parmesan cheese

Instructions:

1. Set oven to 425 degrees Fahrenheit. Add 1 tablespoon of oil to the bottom of an 8-inch square baking dish.
2. Dry the scallops off and place them in the dish in a single layer. Add salt and pepper to taste over the scallops.
3. Mix the melted butter, lemon juice, and shallot in a small bowl. Over the scallops, spread the butter mixture. Panko, Parmesan, parsley, and the remaining 2 tablespoons of oil are combined in the same bowl. Over the scallops, evenly distribute the panko mixture.
4. Bake for 10 to 15 minutes or until the topping is golden brown and the scallops are opaque. Serve warm.

Nutritional Info:

Calories: 281 kcal Fat: 18 g Protein: 17 g Carbs: 13 g Sugar: 1 g Sodium: 470 mg

47. Clam Chowder

Prep Time: 5 minutes

Cook Time: 4 hours

Servings: 6

Ingredients:

- 1/8 teaspoon ground black pepper
- 1 1/2 teaspoons of dried thyme
- 1 teaspoon red wine vinegar
- 3 teaspoons of dry sherry
- 3 tablespoons of cornstarch
- 1 cup of vegetable broth
- 1 cup carrots (chopped)
- 1 1/2 cups of onions (chopped)
- 1 1/2 cups red potatoes (chopped)
- 1 1/2 cups of celery (chopped

- 1 1/4 cups water
- 1 scallion green (chopped)
- 1 bottle of clam juice
- 2 pieces of turkey bacon (cooked)
- 1 can of fat-free milk
- 2 cans of clam (chopped)

Instructions:

1. Celery, onions, potatoes, carrots, water, clam juice, broth, thyme, and pepper should be added to a 3 1/2- or 4-quart slow cooker.
2. Cover the pot and cook on low heat for 7 hours or on high heat for 3 1/2 hours.
3. Switch to high heat if currently using low heat. Combine cornstarch and evaporated milk in a medium bowl. Add sherry (if preferred), the milk mixture, and the clams to the cooker. Cook with the lid on for a further 30 to 60 minutes or until the edge is bubbling. Just before serving, stir in the vinegar. If preferred, top each plate with green onion and bacon.

Nutritional Info:

Calories: 222 kcal Fat: 2 g Protein: 25 g Carbs: 26 g Sugar: 10 g Sodium: 599 mg

48. Crab Louie Salad

Prep Time: 45 minutes

Cook Time: 5 minutes

Servings: 4

Ingredients:

- 1 teaspoon horseradish
- 1 teaspoon lemon juice
- 1 tablespoon dill pickle relish
- 2 tablespoons Dried dill
- 1/2 cup cucumber

- 1/2 cup ketchup
- 1/2 cup of mayonnaise
- 1/2 cup black olives
- 1/4 cup of red onions
- 1/4 cup of minced yellow onion
- 1 garlic clove
- 1 green lettuce
- 1 ripe avocado
- 2 scallions
- 2 tomatoes
- 2 hard-boiled eggs
- 2 celery stalks
- 6 ounces of sautéed crabmeat
- 8 asparagus spears

Instructions:

1. Combine the mayonnaise, ketchup, relish, garlic, dill, lemon juice and horseradish.
2. In a big saucepan with a steamer basket attached, bring 1 inch of water to a boil. Put an ice-filled dish close to the stove. When the asparagus is tender-crisp, add it to the pot, cover it, and steam for 3 to 5 minutes. Go to the cold bath after that. Drain and pat dry.
3. On a serving tray, arrange the lettuce. Place the avocado, celery, scallions, cucumber, eggs, tomatoes, red onion, asparagus, and olives, on top. Add crabmeat over top and drizzle with half the dressing. If desired, garnish with lemon slices.

Nutritional Info:

Calories: 325 kcal Fat: 23 g Protein: 15 g Carbs: 19 g Sugar: 8 g Sodium: 603mg

49. Pita Bread Salmon Sandwich

Prep Time: 5 minutes

Cook Time: 5 minutes

Servings: 1

Ingredients:

- 1/2 teaspoon horseradish
- 2 teaspoons Lemon juice
- 2 tablespoons of plain yogurt
- 2 tablespoons dill
- 1/2 cup watercress
- 3 ounces of canned salmon
- 1/2 6-inch pita bread

Instructions:

1. Salmon is added after the yogurt, dill, lemon juice, and horseradish are combined in a small bowl. Place the salmon salad and watercress inside the pita half.

Nutritional Info:

Calories: 239 kcal Fat: 7 g Protein: 24 g Carbs: 19 g Sugar: 3 g Sodium: 510 mg

50. Balacao Guisado

Prep Time: 5 minutes

Cook Time: 45 minutes

Servings: 4

Ingredients:

- 1/2 teaspoon Salt
- 1 teaspoon Oregano,
- 2 tablespoons olive oil,
- 1 tablespoon capers
- 2 tablespoons of green olives
- 1 chopped medium onion
- 1 pound of flaky white fish (cut)
- 1 avocado (chopped)
- 1 can Diced tomatoes
- 1 pepper (chopped)
- 4 minced garlic cloves
- 1/2 cup water
- 1/4 cup fresh cilantro

Instructions:

1. Over medium heat, add oil to a sizable high-sided pan or Dutch oven. Add the onion and simmer for about two minutes, stirring periodically, until soft. Add the garlic and stir for one minute.

2. Stir together the fish, tomatoes, olives, capers, oregano, chili pepper, cilantro, and salt. The mixture may need up to 1/2 cup of water if it appears dry. For 20 minutes, simmer with a cover

on. Get rid of the heat. Serve with avocado as a garnish when heated or at room temperature (if using).

Nutritional Info:

Calories: 189 kcal Fat: 8 g Protein: 20 g Carbs: 8.5 g Sugar: 3 g Sodium: 758 mg

---

51. Walnut Rosemary Salmon

Prep Time: 10 minutes

Cook Time: 10 minutes

Servings: 4

Ingredients:

- 1/2 teaspoon of honey
- 1/4 teaspoon Lemon zest
- 1/4 teaspoon of red pepper flakes
- 1 teaspoon Extra virgin olive oil
- 1 teaspoon chopped rosemary
- 2 teaspoons of Dijon mustard
- 1/2 tablespoon salt
- 3 tablespoons Panko breadcrumbs
- 3 tablespoons of walnuts
- 1 olive oil spray
- 1 minced garlic clove
- 1 skinless salmon fillet
- 1/8 cup lemon juice
- A handful of lemon wedges

Instructions:

1. Set oven to 425 degrees Fahrenheit. Use parchment paper to line a big baking sheet with a rim.

In a small bowl, mix the garlic, mustard, lemon juice, lemon zest, honey rosemary, salt, and red pepper flakes. In a different small bowl, mix the panko, walnuts, and oil.

2. On the prepared baking sheet, put the fish. After applying the mustard mixture to the fish, sprinkle the panko mixture over it and press firmly to help it stick. Apply cooking spray sparingly.

3. Depending on thickness, bake the fish for 8 to 12 minutes or until it flakes easily with a fork.

4. Top with parsley and, if preferred, serve with lemon wedges.

Nutritional Info:

Calories: 222 kcal Fat: 12 g Protein: 24 g Carbs: 4 g Sugar: 1 g Sodium: 256 mg

52. Korean Grilled Mackerel

Prep Time: 5 minutes

Cook Time: 1 hour

Servings: 4

Ingredients:

- 1 teaspoon grated ginger

- 1 tablespoon Canola oil
- 1 tablespoon of soy sauce
- 2 tablespoons Korean chili paste
- 2 tablespoons Rice vinegar
- 2 whole mackerel

Instructions:

1. In a small bowl, combine the ginger, oil, soy sauce, vinegar, and chili paste and whisk to combine. Put 2 tablespoons of the marinade in a small basin and reserve.
2. Each fish may be opened like a book to reveal the meat. Spread the leftover marinade over the flesh and place in a big skillet or on a baking sheet. For 30 to 1 hour, let the food marinate in the refrigerator.
3. Prepare a charcoal fire or preheat the grill to high for about 20 minutes before one is ready to start grilling.
4. Clean and properly oil the grill rack using a brush. For 3 minutes, grill the fish with the flesh side down. With a large spatula, turn the fish over, brush the remaining marinade over it, and cook for an additional 3 to 4 minutes or until the center is opaque.

Nutritional Info:

Calories: 221 kcal Fat: 6 g Protein: 36 g Carbs: e g Sugar: 0.3 g Sodium: 612 mg

53. Tuna, White Bean and Dill Salad

Prep Time: 30 minutes

Cook Time: 2 hours

Servings: 4

Ingredients:

- 1 teaspoon of honey Dijon mustard
- 1/8 tablespoon salt
- 1 1/8 tablespoons of dried dill
- 2 tablespoons of light mayo

- 2 tablespoons apple cider vinegar
- 2 tablespoons Olive oil
- 3 tablespoons
- 1 sprig of fresh dill
- 1 can of white kidney beans
- 2 cans of solid white tuna
- 2 cups of cooked beets
- 3 cups of red onion
- 6 cups Fresh baby spinach

Instructions:

1. In a big bowl, mix beans, tuna, and onion. In a small dish, combine the lemon-pepper seasoning, 3 tablespoons of mustard, 1 tablespoon of mayonnaise, 1 tablespoon of vinegar, and 1 teaspoon of dried dill to make the dressing. Toss lightly to coat after adding dressing to the tuna mixture. For two to four hours, cover and chill.

2. Make the vinaigrette in a little screw-top jar, combine the oil, salt, 1/8 teaspoon dried dill, 1 tablespoon vinegar, and 1 teaspoon mustard. Wrap tightly and shake. In a big bowl, combine spinach and beets. Pour vinaigrette over the spinach mixture and toss to coat before serving.

3. Four dishes should be filled with the spinach mixture for serving. The tuna mixture is on top. Add some freshly chopped dill and/or pepper, if preferred.

Nutritional Info:

Calories: 296 kcal Fat: 11 g Protein: 20 g Carbs: 25 g Sugar: 7 g Sodium: 550 mg

54. Fish Curry

Prep Time: 5 minutes

Cook Time: 35 minutes

Servings: 6

Ingredients:

- 1 teaspoon salt
- 1/4 teaspoon dried
- 1 teaspoon of Scotch bonnet pepper
- 2 tablespoons Curry powder
- 3 tablespoons Canola oil
- 1 onion
- 1 green bell pepper
- 2 minced garlic cloves
- 1 can of coconut milk
- 2 pounds Mahi-mahi fillets

- 3 finely sliced scallions

Instructions:

1. Put a big skillet with medium heat to heat the oil. After one minute, add curry powder. Add the thyme, onion, bell pepper, garlic, and chile pepper. About 2 minutes of stirring cooking will provide fragrant food. Simmer after adding coconut milk. Then add fish and scallions, and simmer the mixture for 5 to 7 minutes with the lid on. Add salt and serve right away.

Nutritional Info:

Calories: 264 kcal Fat: 12 g Protein: 29 g Carbs:6 g Sugar: 1 g Sodium: 540 mg

55. Shrimp Piccata with Zucchini Noodles

Prep Time: 5 minutes

Cook Time: 35 minutes

Servings: 4

Ingredients:

- 1/2 teaspoon salt
- 2 teaspoons parsley
- 1 tablespoon Cornstarch
- 2 tablespoons Butter
- 2 tablespoons of extra virgin olive oil
- 3 tablespoons rinsed capers
- 1 pound of shrimp
- 2 minced garlic cloves
- 6 medium zucchini
- 1 cup of chicken broth
- 1/3 cup white wine
- 1/4 cup of Lemon juice

Instructions:

1. Slice the zucchini lengthwise into long, thin strands or strips using a vegetable peeler or a spiral slicer. When one gets to the seeds in the middle, stop (the seeds make the noodles fall apart). Put the noodles of zucchini in a sieve and season with salt. After 15 to 30 minutes, let drain, then gently squeeze to get rid of any extra water.

2. In the meantime, warm 1 tablespoon oil and 1 tablespoon butter in a big skillet over medium-high heat. For 30 seconds, while stirring, add the garlic. Add the shrimp and stir for one minute.

3. In a small bowl, combine the cornstarch and broth. Add wine, lemon juice, and capers to the shrimp. Simmer for 4 to 5 minutes, stirring periodically, until the shrimp are barely cooked through. Get rid of the heat.

4. A sizable nonstick skillet with the remaining 1 tablespoon of oil should be heated over medium-high heat. Add the zucchini noodles and stir gently for three minutes or until heated. Sprinkle parsley on top of the zucchini noodles before adding the shrimp and sauce.

Nutritional Info:

Calories: 271 kcal Fat: 15 g Protein: 24 g Carbs: 12 g Sugar: 6 g Sodium: 516 mg

Chapter 6: Meat and Poultry Recipes

56. Birria

Prep Time: 20 minutes

Cook Time: 3 hours 15 minutes

Servings: 12

Ingredients:

- 1 teaspoon of assorted spices
- 1 tablespoon salt
- ¼ onion
- 3 pounds of beef stew meat in cube form
- 6 bay leaves
- 5 dried Anaheim peppers
- 5 Guajillo peppers
- Sufficient water (to cover)

Instructions:

1. Put the Anaheim and guajillo peppers in a pot, cover them with water, and bring the pot to a boil. Turn the heat down to medium-low and cook the meat until it is soft, which should take around 15 minutes. Set aside to cool for 5 minutes.

2. Put the chilies and the water in a blender, then add the onion, the spice mixture, and the salt. Combine until there are no lumps.

3. Put the stew meat in a big pot, toss in the pureed chile mixture, and then throw in some bay leaves. Cook the meat over low to medium heat for anywhere between three and five hours or until it is extremely soft.

Nutritional Info:

Calories: 159 kcal Fat: 7 g Protein: 21 g Carbs: 3 g Sugar: 1 g Sodium: 630 mg

57. Beef Stroganoff

Prep Time: 30 minutes

Cook Time: 4 hours

Servings: 6

Ingredients:

- ½ teaspoon salt
- 1/2 teaspoon of dried oregano
- 1/4 teaspoon ground black pepper
- 1 4/5 teaspoons dried thyme
- 2 teaspoons vegetable oil
- 2 teaspoons of flour
- 1/3 cup dry beef broth
- 2 cups of fresh mushrooms
- 2 cups of hot noodles
- 1 onion
- 1 bay leaf
- 1 pound of beef stew meat
- 1 can beef broth
- 1 container of light sour cream
- 1 fresh parsley
- 2 garlic cloves

Instructions:

1. Remove excess fat from the beef. Cube the beef to a thickness of one inch. Cook the beef until it is browned in a large skillet by cooking it half at a time in hot oil over medium heat. Remove any excess fat.

2. Place the mushrooms, onion, garlic, oregano, salt, thyme, pepper, and the bay leaf in a slow

cooker that is either 3 1/2 or 4 quarts in capacity. Add beef. In the cooker, pour the broth and sherry all over the ingredients.

3. Cook, covered, on the low-heat setting for eight to ten hours or on the high-heat setting for four to five hours. Take out the bay leaf and throw it away.

4. Change the setting to high heat if previously using the low heat setting. Mix together the sour cream and cornstarch in a bowl of medium size. Whisk in about 1 cup of the hot cooking liquid in a gradual manner while adding it to the sour cream mixture. The cooker should be stirred with the sour cream mixture. Continue to cook, covered, for about another half an hour or until the sauce has thickened. Serve over hot noodles that have been cooked. If one so desires, top each portion with some chopped parsley.

Nutritional Info:

Calories: 257 kcal Fat: 10 g Protein: 26 g Carbs: 14 g Sugar: 3 g Sodium: 312 mg

58. Creamy Tuscan Chicken

Prep Time: 5 minutes

Cook Time: 45 minutes

Servings: 4

Ingredients:

- 1 teaspoon salt
- 1 teaspoon dried oregano
- 1 teaspoon Black pepper
- 1 tablespoon of olive oil
- 3 tablespoons of butter
- 3 whole garlic cloves, chopped
- 4 chicken breasts
- 1 1/2 ounces of cherry tomatoes
- 1/2 cup of heavy cream
- 1/4 cup Lemon wedges
- 3 cups chopped baby spinach
- A handful of Parmesan cheese

Instructions:

1. In a skillet over medium heat, heat oil. After adding the chicken, season it with salt, pepper, and oregano before serving. Cook until golden and no longer pink, 8 minutes per side. Remove from skillet and set aside.

2. In the same skillet over medium heat, melt butter. After approximately a minute, stir in the garlic and heat until the aroma is released. To taste, season with salt and pepper after adding cherry tomatoes. Once the tomatoes have reached the point where they are ready to burst, add the spinach and continue to simmer until it begins to wilt.

3. Add the heavy cream and parmesan cheese while stirring, then bring the sauce up to a simmer. Turn the heat down to low and simmer the sauce for about three minutes or until it has shrunk in volume significantly. Place the chicken back into the pan, and continue to cook for another 5 to 7 minutes or until it is fully heated.

4. The fourth step is to serve the dish with lemon wedges.

Nutritional Info:

Calories: 380 kcal Fat: 14 g Protein: 29 g Carbs: 5 g Sugar: 2 g Sodium: 250 mg

59. Gyro Meat

Prep Time: 15 minutes

Cook Time: 45 minutes

Servings: 10

Ingredients:

- 1 teaspoon of dried thyme
- 1 teaspoon of black pepper
- 1 teaspoon of oregano
- 1 teaspoon of dried rosemary
- 1 teaspoon dried marjoram
- 1 teaspoon of cumin
- ¼ teaspoon sea salt
- 1 tablespoon of garlic
- 1/2 of an onion
- 1 kg of ground lamb
- 1 kg of minced beef

Instructions:

1. In a food processor, chop the onion until it reaches a very fine consistency. To extract the juice from the onions, place them in the middle of a towel, gather up the ends of the cloth, and squeeze.
2. In a large bowl, combine the onions, lamb, beef, garlic, cumin, oregano, marjoram, rosemary, salt, thyme, and pepper. Use hands to mix the ingredients thoroughly. Cover and place in the refrigerator for one to two hours to let the flavors meld together.
3. Turn the temperature in the oven up to 325 degrees F. (165 degrees C).

4. Put the beef mixture into the food processor, and pulse it for approximately a minute or until the meat is finely minced and the texture feels tacky. Transfer to a loaf pan measuring 7 by 4 inches and firmly pack down to ensure that there are no air spaces.

5. To prevent the food from sticking, line a big roasting pan with a damp kitchen towel. Put the loaf pan in the middle of the towel-lined roasting pan, and then move the whole thing into the oven once it has been prepared. Place the loaf pan inside the roasting pan and carefully pour boiling water into the roasting pan until the water reaches the halfway point of the loaf pan.

6. Using a meat thermometer, bake the gyro meat in the oven that has been prepared for 45 minutes to 1 hour, or until the middle of the meat is no longer pink and the internal temperature reads 165 degrees Fahrenheit (75 degrees C).

7. Remove any excess fat that has formed, then allow the meat to cool slightly before slicing it thinly and serving it.

Nutritional Info:

Calories: 179 kcal Fat: 12 g Protein: 16 g Carbs: 2 g Sugar: 1 g Sodium: 97 mg

60. White Sauce Breast Chicken

Prep Time: 5 minutes

Cook Time: 25 minutes

Servings: 5

Ingredients:

- ¼ teaspoon onion granules
- 1 teaspoon Dijon mustard
- 2 tablespoons butter
- 2 2/4 tablespoons flour
- 3 tablespoons of olive oil
- 3 tablespoons of light sour cream
- 4 tablespoons of white wine
- 1½ cups light milk
- 1/2 crumbled stock vegetables
- 4 chicken breasts
- Black pepper (to taste)
- Salt (to taste)

Instructions:

1. The chicken breasts should be fried for two to three minutes on each side in a large shallow pan over medium heat. The oil should be heated to three tablespoons (or until golden brown). Place the chicken on a plate, cover it, and put it to the side for a moment (leave the juices, if any, in the pan).

2. In the same saucepan, melt the butter over low heat before adding the flour and whisking the mixture until it forms a thick paste that is smooth (this is roux).

3. After adding the wine and giving it a good stir, add half of the milk, turn the heat up, and continue whisking until the sauce begins to thicken. Continue whisking the mixture while adding stock cube, milk mustard, onion grains, and pepper to taste. Keep doing this until the sauce begins to thicken and bubble up. After combining the fromage frais with a whisk, it is time to taste the sauce and make any necessary adjustments to the seasoning.

4. After coating the chicken in the sauce, return it to the pan, cover it, and reduce the heat to low.

Simmer for 10 to 15 minutes or until the chicken is fully cooked. If necessary, add a splash of water, give it a stir, and serve it right away.

Nutritional Info:

Calories: 387 kcal Fat: 19 g Protein: 16 g Carbs: 8 g Sugar: 4 g Sodium: 364 mg

61. Beef and Broccoli Stir Fry

Prep Time: 10 minutes

Cook Time: 15 minutes

Servings: 4

Ingredients:

- 1/4 teaspoon salt
- 1 tablespoon of sesame seeds
- 1 tablespoon of sesame oil
- 2 tablespoons of cornstarch
- 1 pound of sirloin steak
- 2 garlic cloves
- 1/2 cup of water
- 1/2 cup vegetable broth
- 1/4 cup soy sauce
- 4 cups of broccoli florets

Instructions:

1. Get all of the ingredients together.
2. To ensure that the sirloin steak remains tender after being sliced, cut it across the grain into thin strips.
3. Place the beef strips inside a large plastic bag, then add 1 tablespoon of cornstarch and a pinch of salt, and seal the bag. To thoroughly combine the ingredients and ensure that the beef is evenly coated, shake the bag containing the beef.

4. In a large skillet or wok, bring the sesame oil to a warm temperature over medium-high heat. After adding the beef, stir-fry it for about four minutes or until the color has completely disappeared. Take the beef out of the pan, place it in a bowl, and put it to the side for a moment.

5. Cook the garlic in the skillet or wok for one minute or until it has developed a strong flavor but has not yet become burnt. Take the time and add the water as well as the broccoli. Broccoli should be cooked for an additional 4 to 5 minutes until it turns a bright green color and becomes more tender.

6. During the time that the broccoli is cooking, combine the remaining 1 tablespoon of cornstarch, the vegetable broth, and the soy sauce in a small dish and whisk until smooth. The beef should be returned to the skillet along with this soy sauce.

7. Continue to cook the entire mixture for an additional minute or two or until the sauce has reached the desired consistency. Take the dish away from the heat.

8. Place the finished dish in a serving bowl and top with toasted sesame seeds, if desired.

9. Enjoy!

Nutritional Info:

Calories: 388 kcal Fat: 20 g Protein: 36 g Carbs: 13 g Sugar: 26 g Sodium: 1220 mg

62. Meatloaf with Vegetables

Prep Time: 15 minutes

Cook Time: 1 hour 15 minutes

Servings: 6

Ingredients:

- 2 tablespoons Dijon mustard
- 1/2 cup of finely chopped green pepper
- 1/2 cup of ketchup, cut into thirds
- 1/4 of a cup of minced onion
- 1 cup of whole wheat bread crumbs
- 2 large egg whites (beaten)

- 1 pound of lean ground beef
- 1 pinch of black pepper

Instructions:

1. Turn the oven temperature up to 350 degrees F.
2. Keep 2 tablespoons of the ketchup separate.
3. Mix the remaining ingredients in a large bowl until they are evenly distributed throughout the bowl.
4. Spray a loaf pan with cooking spray that prevents sticking. Make a loaf with the hands out of the meat mixture, and place it in the pan designated for loaves. Spread the remaining ketchup on top.
5. Bake for 1 hour and 15 minutes or until the center is thoroughly cooked through. Check it after the first hour.
6. Take the meatloaf out of the oven and set it aside. Let it rest for 5 minutes before serving.

Nutritional Info:

Calories: 149 kcal Fat: 21 g Protein: 74 g Carbs: 397 g Sugar: 177 g Sodium: 644 mg

63. Spinach and Turkey Lasagna

Prep Time: 25 minutes

Cook Time: 100 minutes

Servings: 6

Ingredients:

- 1/4 teaspoon salt
- 1/4 teaspoon pepper
- 1 tablespoon olive oil
- 2 cups chopped onion
- 1 1/2 cups part-skim ricotta cheese
- 1/2 cup shredded part-skim mozzarella cheese
- 1/3 cup of grated Parmesan
- 3 cups jarred marinara sauce
- 1/4 cup of parsley
- 1 package of frozen spinach
- 2 cloves of garlic
- 2 egg whites of large eggs
- 3/4 of a pound of ground turkey breast
- 12 lasagna noodles

Instructions:

1. Put the oven temperature to 375 degrees Fahrenheit.
2. Warm the olive oil in a large skillet with high sides, add the onion, and cook it for 6 to 7 minutes, stirring it occasionally, until it has softened. Cook the garlic for one minute after adding it. After adding the turkey, cook it for 4 to 5 minutes, breaking it up with a spoon, until it is no longer pink and is fully cooked through. After adding the marinara, bring the mixture to a boil, then reduce the heat and let it simmer for two to three minutes. Take the pan off the heat and let it cool down a little bit.

3. In a large bowl, combine the ricotta cheese, spinach, and parsley, along with the egg whites, salt, and pepper.

4. Spread half a cup of sauce across the bottom of a lasagna pan that measures 14 inches by 11 inches. Arrange three lasagna noodles in a single layer across the base of the dish. Spread approximately three-quarters of a cup of sauce over the noodles. Spread the ricotta and spinach mixture, which amounts to 2/3 cup, evenly over the sauce. Layers should be repeated a total of three times.

5. Place three more noodles on top, along with the remaining three-quarters of a cup of sauce. Mozzarella and Parmesan cheese should be sprinkled on top. Bake for 45 minutes with the dish covered in foil in a loose manner. Take off the foil and continue baking for another 10 to 15 minutes or until the cheese is bubbling. After cutting it into squares, serve it.

Nutritional Info:

Calories: 286 kcal Fat: 9 g Protein: 23 g Carbs: 31 g Sugar: 4 g Sodium: 547mg

64. Chicken Pot Pie

Prep Time: 20 minutes

Cook Time: 50 minutes

Servings: 8

Ingredients:

- ⅓ cup all-purpose flour
- ½ teaspoon salt
- ½ cup sliced celery
- 1 and ¾ cups chicken broth
- ⅓ cup chopped onion
- 1 cup sliced carrot
- ⅔ cup of milk
- ¼ teaspoon celery seed
- 1-pound chicken breast
- ¼ teaspoon black pepper
- ⅓ cup butter
- 2 non-baked pie crusts

Instructions:

1. Turn the temperature in the oven up to 400 degrees F.
2. In a saucepan, combine the carrots, celery, peas, and chicken; add enough water to cover the ingredients, and bring to a simmer. After 15 minutes at a rolling boil, turn off the heat and drain the liquid.
3. In a separate pot, over moderate heat, melt the butter. Do this while the chicken is cooking. After adding the onion, continue to cook it for 5 to 7 minutes or until it has become transparent. Mix in the salt, celery seed, pepper, and flour until it is evenly distributed. While stirring constantly, add the chicken broth and milk. Turn the heat down to medium-low and simmer the mixture until it becomes thick, anywhere from 5 to 10 minutes. Take the pan off the warmth, and set it aside.
4. In the pie crust's bottom layer, arrange the chicken and vegetables. Pour the hot liquid mixture over the top. Cover with the top crust, pinch the edges together to seal and remove any excess dough before serving. Cut vents in the top crust in the form of several tiny slits so that the steam can escape.

5. Bake for 30 to 35 minutes in an oven that has been preheated until the pastry is golden brown and the filling is bubbling. Wait for the dish to cool for ten minutes before serving.

Nutritional Info:

Calories: 412 kcal Fat: 24 g Protein: 18 g Carbs: 30 g Sugar: 3 g Sodium: 517 mg

65. Paleo Tomato Chicken Curry with Cauliflower Rice

Prep Time: 10 minutes

Cook Time: 30 minutes

Servings: 4

Ingredients:

- 3/4 teaspoon salt
- 1/4 teaspoon pepper
- 2 teaspoons of fresh ginger
- 2 tablespoons of curry powder
- 2 tablespoons of clarified butter
- 1/4 cup cilantro
- 1 yellow onion
- 1 package of cauliflower rice (cooked)
- 1 can of crushed tomatoes
- 1 can of light coconut milk
- 2 garlic cloves
- 1 1/4 pounds of chicken breast

Instructions:

1. Melt ghee in a skillet over moderate heat. Cook the chicken, occasionally stirring, until the first half of the pieces are browned. Remove from skillet and set aside. Repeat the process with the other half of the chicken. After adding the onion, jalapeno, garlic, and ginger to the skillet, continue to cook while stirring for approximately 5 minutes or until the vegetables have

become softer. After about a minute of constant stirring, the curry powder will become fragrant and be ready to be added. Bring the tomatoes and the coconut milk to a boil after adding them. Add salt and pepper.

2. Turn the heat down to low and simmer the sauce for 15 to 20 minutes, stirring the chicken and any accumulated juices during the last 5 minutes of cooking. The sauce should become slightly thicker and reduced. Mix in the quarter cup of chopped cilantro.

3. Serve atop cauliflower rice with cilantro.

Nutritional Info:

Calories: 380 kcal Fat: 13 g Protein: 29 g Carbs: 13 g Sugar: 26 g Sodium: 30 mg

66. Tandoori Chicken

Prep Time: 30 minutes

Cook Time: 15 minutes

Servings: 8

Ingredients:

- ½ tsp chili powder
- 1/3 teaspoon of garam masala

- 1/4 teaspoon of turmeric
- 1/4 teaspoon of ground cumin
- 4 teaspoons paprika
- 8 tablespoons of lemon juice
- 1 ginger
- 1 vegetable oil
- 2 red onions
- 4 garlic cloves
- 16 skinless chicken thighs
- 300ml Greek yogurt

Instructions:

1. In a large dish with a shallow bottom, combine the lemon juice, paprika, and chopped red onions. After cutting each thigh of the chicken three times, turn them over in the juice and set them aside for ten minutes.

2. Combine all of the ingredients for the marinade in a separate bowl, then pour it over the chicken. After giving everything a thorough mix, cover it and place it in the refrigerator for at least an hour. One has up to a day's head start to complete this task.

3. Preheat the barbecue. Raise the pieces of chicken onto a rack that is set atop a baking sheet. Brush on some oil, then place on the grill for about eight minutes per side or until the surface is lightly charred and the center is no longer raw.

Nutritional Info:

Calories: 171 kcal Fat: 7 g Protein: 24 g Carbs: 4 g Sugar: 2 g Sodium: 1 mg

67. Shiitake Mushroom Chicken Ramen

Prep Time: 15 minutes

Cook Time: 10 minutes

Servings: 2

Ingredients:

- 1/2 teaspoon of black pepper
- 1/2 teaspoon of salt
- 1 teaspoon of chili powder.
- 2/4 teaspoon of ginger powder
- 1 1/2 tablespoons of soy sauce
- 1 teaspoon of powdered garlic
- 1/2 tablespoon of minced garlic
- 2 tablespoons avocado oil
- 2 Organic Servings of Brown Rice
- 4 ounces of sliced shiitake mushrooms
- 1/2 pound of chicken thighs
- 4 cups of chicken bone broth

Instructions:

1. Prepare the ramen noodles in accordance with the instructions on the package, then set them aside. In order to prevent the noodles from sticking together while the chicken and broth are being prepared, those using brown rice ramen should ensure that they soak them in a very small amount of cold water before serving.

2. Salt, pepper, garlic powder, ground ginger, and chili powder should be mixed together in a little bowl. To evenly distribute the seasoning on the chicken, place the thighs in a medium bowl along with the seasoning mix, and use tongs to mix the ingredients.

3. In a large Dutch oven or deep skillet, bring one tablespoon of oil up to temperature over medium heat. Include shiitake mushrooms and garlic that has been minced. Continue to stir

the mixture occasionally while it cooks for about 5 minutes. Take out of the pan and put to the side.

4. In the same pan, add the last tablespoon of oil to the mixture. After adding the chicken thighs, continue to cook them for another 5 or 6 minutes over medium heat until they begin to brown. After the flip, continue cooking for another 5 minutes or until an internal temperature of 165 degrees Fahrenheit is reached. Take the chicken out of the pan and put it to the side for later. There should be some brown bits left in the pan from the chicken that one cooked. Once it has cooled, the chicken should be cut into strips.

5. The same hot pan should be placed over medium heat, and one cup of the chicken broth should be added to it. Using a wooden spoon, scrape the bits from the bottom of the pan as they become loose. After approximately sixty seconds, pour in the remaining broth along with the soy sauce. Turn the heat down to a low simmer and cook for ten minutes.

6. Put the noodles, mushrooms, and chicken into individual bowls. Top each bowl with two cups of broth, and then sprinkle on the toppings.

Nutritional Info:

Calories: 610 kcal Fat: 19 g Protein: 48 g Carbs: 61 g Sugar: 3 g Sodium: 30 mg

68. Pumpkin Chilli Chicken

Prep Time: 45 minutes

Cook Time: 2 hours

Servings: 4

Ingredients:

- 1 teaspoon of ground chili peppers
- 1 1/2 teaspoons salt
- 1/2 teaspoon freshly ground black pepper
- 1 1/2 teaspoons of cumin seed powder
- 2 tablespoons olive oil
- 1 large onion
- 1 minced chili pepper
- 4 whole garlic cloves chopped
- 1 bay leaf
- 1 cup of pumpkin puree
- 2 cans of cannellini beans
- 4 cups of chicken
- 4 cups of chicken broth
- 3-4 cups of corn
- 6 slices of Cheddar

Instructions:

1. In a Dutch oven, bring the olive oil up to temperature over medium flame. After adding the onion and Fresno, continue cooking while frequently stirring for 5 to 6 minutes or until the onions have become translucent and tender. After stirring in the garlic, chili powder, cumin, and bay leaf, continue cooking the mixture for one to two minutes or until the spices begin to release their aroma. After adding the pumpkin puree, continue to stir and cook for another two to three minutes or until the mixture begins to bubble and brown slightly.

2. Add the chicken that has been shredded, then season it with salt and pepper. After pouring in the chicken broth, scrape the bottommost of the pot with a wooden spoon to remove any browned bits that have accumulated there. Bring to a low boil, then reduce the heat to maintain a simmer, and continue cooking for one hour, stirring the mixture occasionally. After stirring in the beans and corn, continue cooking the chili in a covered pot over low heat for about 30 minutes or until the liquid has evaporated and the chili has reached the desired consistency.

3. Using a cookie cutter in the shape of a pumpkin, cut the cheese slices into the shape of pumpkins. Give each pumpkin the appearance of a jack-o'-lantern by carving eyes, a nose, and a mouth into it with a paring knife. Put some of the chili in individual bowls and then top each with a cheese pumpkin. Greek yogurt, sliced scallions, and tortilla chips should be served alongside this dish.

Nutritional Info:

Calories: 318 kcal Fat: 9 g Protein: 22 g Carbs: 38 g Sugar: 11 g Sodium: 1030 mg

69. Stuffed Chicken Breast

Prep Time: 5 minutes

Cook Time: 25 minutes

Servings: 1

Ingredients:

- 1/4 teaspoon of curry powder
- 1 teaspoon of chopped sundried tomato
- 1/4 teaspoon of paprika
- 1 teaspoon of salt.
- 1 skinless chicken breast
- 1 clove of garlic
- 1 ounce of low-fat mozzarella
- 1 artichoke heart
- 5 large basil leaves

Instructions:

1. Put the oven on to 365 degrees Fahrenheit and turn it on. Prepare a baking sheet by lining it with either aluminum foil or parchment paper. Set aside.
2. Make butterfly cuts in the chicken breast. Holding the top of the chicken breast in one hand, guide a sharp knife from the thicker end of the chicken breast, slicing towards the thin end of the chicken breast. Take care not to cut through to the opposite side of the chicken breast.
3. 1 boneless and skinless chicken breast to start.
4. In the meantime, cut the mozzarella cheese into thin slices and the artichoke into shreds. Then cut the tomatoes and basil into thin slices. Chopping the garlic into large pieces. Put everything in a bowl or do it all on the cutting board and mix it together.
5. 1 ounce of low-fat mozzarella, 1 artichoke heart (in water), 1 teaspoon of sundried tomato (dried but not in oil), 5 large basil leaves, and 1 garlic clove
6. Place a dollop of the mozzarella mixture on one side of the open chicken breast that has been butterflied, and then spread it out evenly across the open chicken breast.
7. Cover the stuffing by folding the opposite side of these chicken breast back into their original form. Doing so will create a sandwich with the stuffing located in the middle of the two halves of the chicken breast. Put some toothpicks through the top and bottom layers of the chicken breast that has been opened so that it is secure.
8. Place the stuffed chicken breasts on the baking sheet that has been previously prepared. Add a dash of ground black pepper, curry powder, and paprika to taste.
9. 1/8 teaspoon ground black pepper, 1/8 teaspoon paprika, and 1/8 teaspoon curry powder
10. When the chicken breasts reach an internal temperature of 165 degrees Fahrenheit, the chicken is baked in the oven that has been preheated. The use of an instant-read meat thermometer is the method that yields the most accurate results when testing for doneness. Put the thermometer for the meat in the thickest part of the breast. The chicken is cooked all the way through when the thermometer registers 165 degrees Fahrenheit. One also has the option of using a knife to pierce holes in the chicken. When the chicken is cooked properly, the juices should be clear.
11. Take the chicken breast away from the heat and let it stand undisturbed for five minutes so that the juices can redistribute themselves throughout the chicken. Take out the toothpicks,

then serve.

Nutritional Info:

Calories: 223 kcal Fat: 9 g Protein: 32 g Carbs: 5 g Sugar: 2 g Sodium: 317 mg

70. Creamy Mushroom Chicken

Prep Time: 15 minutes

Cook Time: 15 minutes

Servings: 4

Ingredients:

- 2 tablespoons of fresh parsley
- 1/2 cup of full-fat heavy cream
- 4 cups of a variety of mushrooms
- 1/2 ounce of a dry white wine
- 4 to 5 ounces of chicken cutlets

Instructions:

1. Sprinkle chicken with a quarter of a teaspoon of kosher salt and a quarter of a teaspoon of pepper. In a large skillet, bring 1 tablespoon of canola oil up to temperature over medium heat. Cook the chicken for seven to ten minutes in total, turning it over once until it is browned and just cooked through. Place on a plate and set aside.

2. Add one tablespoon of oil and the mushrooms to the pan, then cook for approximately four minutes while stirring the mixture occasionally and allowing the liquid to evaporate. Raise the temperature to high, add the wine, and continue cooking for approximately four minutes or until the liquid has almost completely evaporated. Turn the heat down to medium and stir in the cream along with any chicken juices that may have accumulated, along with a quarter teaspoon each of salt and pepper. Place the chicken back in the pan and turn it over so that it is coated in the sauce. One should serve the chicken with the sauce drizzled over it and some chopped parsley on top.

Nutritional Info:

Calories: 325 kcal Fat: 19 g Protein: 29 g Carbs: 5 g Sugar: 2 g Sodium: 329 mg

Chapter 7: Dessert Recipes

71. Black Bean Fudge Brownies

Prep Time: 10 minutes

Cook Time: 35 unsweetened minutes

Servings: 16

Ingredients:

- 1/2 teaspoon baking soda
- 1/4 teaspoon table salt
- 1 1/2 teaspoons of instant coffee
- 1 1/2 teaspoons vanilla extract
- 3 tablespoons unsalted butter
- 1 can of black beans
- 2 large eggs
- 1/3 cup cocoa powder

- 2/3 cup granulated sugar
- 2/3 cup chocolate chips

Instructions:

1. Prepare the oven to 360 degrees Fahrenheit. Prepare a baking pan measuring 8 by 8 inches by lining it with parchment paper and setting it aside.

2. The black beans should be pureed in the bowl of a food processor on high speed until they are almost completely smooth. Stop the machine and scrape down the sides of the bowl as necessary. After adding the butter and vanilla, process the mixture until it is smooth. Add eggs, then pulse the mixture three to four times to combine. To combine the sugar, coffee, cocoa, baking soda, and salt, pulse the ingredients four to five times. Add chocolate chips, and pulse once or until the mixture is almost completely incorporated.

3. Put the batter into a pan that has been prepared. Bake at 350°F for 26–30 minutes or until set. Let cool while still in the pan on a wire rack.

Nutritional Info:

Calories: 137 kcal Fat: 6 g Protein: 2 g Carbs: 20 g Sugar: 14 g Sodium: 57 mg

72. Zucchini Double Chocolate Bread

Prep Time: 15 minutes

Cook Time: 1 hour

Servings: 12

Ingredients:

- 1/2 teaspoon salt
- 1 1/2 teaspoons vanilla extract
- 1 1/2 teaspoon ground flaxseed
- 1/2 teaspoon baking soda
- 1/2 teaspoon baking powder
- 1 1/4 teaspoons of cinnamon powder
- 1/4 teaspoon of nutmeg powder

- 2 cups white whole-wheat flour
- 1/4 cup Cocoa powder
- 2 cups of zucchini
- 1/3 cup dark chocolate
- 1/2 cup of plain Greek yogurt
- 1/3 cup coconut sugar
- 1/3 cup canola oil
- 1/4 cup (maple syrup
- 2 large eggs

Instructions:

1. Prepare the oven to 350 degrees Fahrenheit (178 degrees Celsius). Spray a loaf pan measuring 9 inches by 5 inches or a square baking pan measuring 8 inches by 20 centimeters with cooking spray. Set aside. Put the cinnamon, cocoa powder, baking powder, baking soda, flour, and nutmeg into a large bowl and sift them all together.

2. In a separate bowl, combine the coconut sugar, oil, yogurt, maple syrup, eggs, and extract by whisking them all together. Mix the dry ingredients with the liquid ones, then add them to the flour mixture and mix until everything is just combined (with a few traces of flour still present). To the mixing bowl, add the zucchini, then stir in the chocolate chips. The batter will have a substantial consistency.

3. After the baking dish has been prepared, the batter should be transferred to it using a spoon, and then the top should be smoothed out using a rubber spatula. Bake the bread for approximately 45 minutes if using a loaf pan and 30 minutes if using an 8-inch square pan until a fork stabbed into the middle of the bread comes out clean. Allow cooling for ten minutes in the pan. After running a knife along the rim of the pan, invert the contents of the pan onto a cooling rack. The leftovers can be stored airtight for up to four days at room temperature if they are tightly wrapped.

Nutritional Info:

Calories: 219 kcal Fat: 3 g Protein: 5 g Carbs: 25 g Sugar: 7 g Sodium: 187 mg

73. Chocolate Tahini Cookies

Prep Time: 15 minutes

Cook Time: 25 minutes

Servings: 12

Ingredients:

- 1/4 teaspoon vanilla extract
- 1 tablespoon tahini
- 1 cup of powdered sugar
- 1/3 cup of unsweetened cocoa powder,
- 2 egg whites from large eggs
- Sprinkle of Salt

Instructions:

1. Prepare two large baking sheets by lining them with parchment paper or silicone mats and heating the oven to 350 degrees Fahrenheit (175 degrees Celsius).
2. Sugar, cocoa, and salt should be mixed together in a sizable bowl. Stir in the egg whites and vanilla extract with a whisk until the batter is completely smooth and thick. In the beginning,

it will appear as though there is no way that it will come together; however, in the end, it does.

3. Whisk the tahini in a small bowl until it is completely smooth, then set it aside.

4. Place twelve even and heaping one-tablespoon scoops of the batter onto each baking sheet, spacing them about two inches (five centimeters) apart. The spoonfuls will immediately spread out across the surface. Tahini should be drizzled over each cookie to the extent of a quarter teaspoon. If one like, sprinkle some coarse sea salt on top. Bake for 12–15 minutes, or until the cookies have cracked and become glossy and the tahini has begun to bubble. Ten minutes of cooling time should be spent on the baking sheets before moving the treats to cool racks.

Nutritional Info:

Calories: 64 kcal Fat: 1 g Protein: 2 g Carbs: 10 g Sugar: 8 g Sodium: 92 mg

74. Oatmeal and Peanut Butter Cookies

Prep Time: 5 minutes

Cook Time: 15 minutes

Servings: 8

Ingredients:

- 1/2 teaspoon vanilla
- 1/4 teaspoon baking soda
- 1 teaspoon of highly refined coconut oil
- 1/2 cup peanut butter
- 1/2 cup pastry flour
- 1/2 cup maple syrup
- 1/4 cup protein powder
- 1 cup rolled oats
- 1 large egg white

Instructions:

1. Prepare the oven to 375 degrees Fahrenheit (190 degrees Celsius). Spray a baking sheet with nonstick cooking spray and set it aside. Coconut oil, peanut butter, maple syrup, egg white, and

vanilla extract should be mixed together in a large bowl. Flour, oats, protein powder, and baking soda should be combined in a low-volume bowl. While stirring, thoroughly combine the dry ingredients in the bowl with the liquid ingredients.

2. Scoop out portions equal to 2 tablespoons, roll them into balls, and then place them on a sheet pan that has been prepared with a gap of 3 inches between each one. Flatten the cookies to a thickness of about half an inch to three-quarters of an inch using the wet palm that one just dipped in running water.

3. Bake for the first six minutes on the bottom rack, then move to the top rack and bake for the remaining twelve minutes. The tops will have a golden brown color, but the centers will have a slight give when pressed. Wait 5 minutes for the food to cool on the pan before transferring it to racks to finish cooling. One can keep the cookies fresh for up to a week in a container with a zip-top bag or airtight container, or they can freeze them for up to two months.

Nutritional Info:

Calories: 230 kcal Fat: 11 g Protein: 7 g Carbs: 28 g Sugar: 14 g Sodium: 83 mg

75. Sweet and Sour Potato Muffins

Prep Time: 10 minutes

Cook Time: 25 minutes

Servings: 9

Ingredients:

- 1/2 teaspoon baking soda
- 1/2 teaspoon baking powder
- 1/4 of a teaspoon of salt
- 1 teaspoon of thyme
- 1/4 cup olive oil
- 1/4 cup maple syrup
- 1 cup roasted sweet potatoes
- 2 cups of pastry flour
- 2 large egg whites (beaten)

Instructions:

1. Turn the temperature on the oven to 350 degrees Fahrenheit (175 degrees Celsius). Prepare a muffin tin by placing a muffin paper in each of the nine cups. Mix the pastry flour, baking soda, baking powder, salt, and thyme together in a large bowl using a whisk to ensure a thorough blending.
2. Mix the pureed sweet potato, egg whites, olive oil, and maple syrup together in a medium bowl using a whisk to ensure a smooth consistency.
3. Mix the mashed sweet potatoes and flour together until they are almost completely incorporated.
4. To portion the batter into the cups, use heaping 1/4 cup scoops, and divide any remaining batter evenly among the cups. If necessary, smooth out the tops.
5. Bake for 20–25 minutes, or until a fork stabbed in the middle of a muffin comes out clean (without any wet batter clinging to it) after being inserted into the oven.
6. Allow to cool on racks, and once it has, store it in the refrigerator, airtight and covered, for up to four days.

Nutritional Info:

Calories: 206 kcal Fat: 7 g Protein: 5 g Carbs: 31 g Sugar: 8 g Sodium: 196 mg

76. Chai Tea Glaze with Pumpkin Spice Bundtlettes

Prep Time: 10 minutes

Cook Time: 20 minutes

Servings: 12

Ingredients:

- 1/2 teaspoon of cardamom powder
- 1 teaspoon of extracted vanilla
- 1/2 teaspoon salt
- 2 teaspoons baking soda
- 2 teaspoons of pumpkin pie spice
- 1 tablespoon of chai tea
- 1 3/4 cups pastry flour
- 1/2 cup packed brown sugar
- 1/4 cup unsalted butter
- 1/4 cup maple syrup
- 1 cup pumpkin puree
- 1/2 cup of powdered sugar
- 1 large egg

Instructions:

1. Preheating the oven to 360 degrees Fahrenheit. Prepare a mini Bundt cake pan with 12 wells by spraying it thoroughly with cooking spray and setting it aside. (If one doesn't have a mini-Bundt pan, they can use a muffin tin instead.)

2. Flour, baking soda, pumpkin pie spice, cardamom, and salt should all be mixed together in a medium bowl using a whisk. Brown sugar and butter are creamed together in a large bowl using a mixer on medium-high speed for three minutes until the mixture is light and fluffy. After adding the egg, give the mixture a good beating. Stir together the pumpkin, maple syrup, and vanilla after adding each ingredient.

3. Using a rubber spatula, gently fold the flour mixture into the pumpkin mixture until it is completely incorporated and there are no traces of flour remaining. Put the batter in the pan that has been prepared and bake it for 18–20 minutes, or until a wooden skewer that has been stabbed into the middle of the cake comes out clean. Put the pan on a cooling rack, and give it ten minutes to cool down completely. After removing the cakes from the pan, place them on a serving tray with the flat side facing down to allow them to cool completely.

4. Sift the powdered sugar for the confection into a low-sided bowl. After adding the chai tea, stir the mixture until it becomes smooth. After drizzling the glaze over the cakes, leave them at room temperature for as long as necessary for the glaze to harden. One can keep it at room temperature for up to four days if they store it in an airtight container.

Nutritional Info:

Calories: 180 kcal Fat: 5 g Protein: 3 g Carbs: 34 g Sugar: 19 g Sodium: 225 mg

77. Avocado Brownies with Frosting

Prep Time: 1 hour

Cook Time: 25 minutes

Servings: 16

Ingredients:

- 1/4 teaspoon of salt
- 1/4 teaspoon of baking soda
- 1 teaspoon lemon juice
- 1/2 cup of cocoa
- 1/2 cup of coconut oil
- 1/4 cup avocado
- 3/4 cup avocado purée
- 3/4 cup unbleached flour
- 1 cup of powdered sugar
- 1 cup caramelized sugar
- 2 large eggs

Instructions:

1. Turn the temperature on the oven to 360 degrees Fahrenheit. Spray a square baking pan that measures 8 inches across with nonstick cooking spray and set it aside.
2. Mix the flour, cocoa, salt, and baking soda together in a large bowl using a whisk.
3. The avocado should be pureed in a food processor until it is completely smooth. After processing the brown sugar, add in the eggs and coconut oil and continue processing until a smooth consistency is reached. The avocado mixture should be scraped into the flour mixture and then stirred to combine everything. Evenly spread the batter in the pan that has been prepared.
4. Bake for twenty to twenty-five minutes, or until the top appears dry and a fork stabbed in the middle of the pan comes out with crumbs attached. Don't overbake. If one prefers a gooey brownie, remove them from the oven while they have just a little bit of moisture left in the middle. It is not necessary to place the brownies in the refrigerator for a couple of hours prior to cutting them, but doing so will make it simpler.
5. In preparation for the icing, put the avocado in the bowl of the food processor and puree it, stopping the machine periodically to scrape down the sides of the bowl. Process the mixture while adding the powdered sugar to create a thick paste. After adding the lemon and scraping

the bowl, process the mixture once more until it is thoroughly combined.

6. When the brownies are done baking, either spread them with frosting and let them stand for 30 minutes before cutting them into squares, or cut them into squares and place a scant tablespoon of frosting on top of each one, as shown in the picture. Make 16 squares measuring 2 inches each. Keep in the refrigerator for up to four days if tightly covered and refrigerated.

Nutritional Info:

Calories: 196 kcal Fat: 9 g Protein: 2 g Carbs: 27 g Sugar: 21 g Sodium: 39 mg

78. Fluff Cake

Prep Time: 5 minutes

Cook Time: 35 minutes

Servings: 12

Ingredients:

- 1 can of crushed pineapple
- 1 box of angel food cake mix
- 1 whipped topping

Instructions:

1. Bring the temperature in the oven up to 3600 degrees. Prepare a pan measuring 9x13 inches with cooking spray, then set it aside.
2. Mix the dry angel food cake mix with the crushed pineapple, including all of the pineapple juice, in a bowl designated for mixing. Stir well.
3. Bake the cake for 35 to 40 minutes in an oven that has been preheated after pouring the batter into the prepared pan. Check on the cake every few minutes after it has been baking for about 30. When it is done cooking all the way through, the cake will have a springy texture, and the top will be golden brown.
4. After allowing it to cool, cut it into squares. Serve with fruit and a topping made of whipped cream. Enjoy!

Nutritional Info:

Calories: 120 kcal Fat: 9 g Protein: 2 g Carbs: 28 g Sugar: 16 g Sodium: 193 mg

79. Vegan Chocolate Pudding

Prep Time: 3 minutes

Cook Time: 2 minutes

Servings: 1

Ingredients:

- 1/4 of a teaspoon of cinnamon
- 1 tablespoon of cacao powder
- 2 tablespoons of maple syrup
- 1 ounce of dark chocolate

Instructions:

1. Create large squares out of the chocolate, and then melt it using the technique of your choice. A) Place the chocolate in the top of a double boiler and heat it over low heat while stirring it frequently until it is almost completely melted. Take the pan off the heat, give it another stir, then let it cool while continuing to stir it every so often for about five minutes. B) Melt the

chocolate in the microwave, beginning with 30 seconds, then continuing for additional increments of 15 seconds while stirring completely after each interval. Heat in the microwave until it has JUST melted. Please allow the mixture to cool while stirring it occasionally for approximately 5 minutes.

2. After removing any liquid that may have settled to the bottom of the tofu container, place the tofu and maple syrup in the bowl of a food processor and pulse until the mixture is smooth. After processing until completely smooth, stop the machine and scrape down the sides before adding the cacao powder and cinnamon. Repeat the procedure. Remove any debris from the sides of the container, then set it aside to cool to room temperature.

3. Put the chocolate that has been melted into the food processor and process it until it is smooth. Remove any residue from the sides. Repeat the procedure. Taste. If it's not sweet enough for the taste, add another tablespoon of maple syrup and process it again until it's completely incorporated.

4. Pour into a serving bowl of moderate size, or divide evenly among four individual serving bowls. One can serve the pudding at room temperature, or one can chill it in the refrigerator for at least an hour before serving. The chocolate pudding can be stored in the refrigerator for up to five days if it is covered.

5. One can eat it as it is, or they can top it with their favorite fruits, berries, nuts, seeds, flaky sea salt, etc.

Nutritional Info:

Calories: 90 kcal Fat: 1 g Protein: 3 g Carbs: 13 g Sugar: 10 g Sodium: 5 mg

80. Chocolate Baked Donuts

Prep Time: 10 minutes

Cook Time: 8 minutes

Servings: 12

Ingredients:

- 1/2 teaspoon
- 1/4 teaspoon salt
- 1 1/4 teaspoons baking powder

- 1 teaspoon vanilla
- 1 1/2 teaspoons of milk
- 1/2 cup granulated sugar
- 1/4 cup mini chocolate chips
- 3/4 of a cup of icing sugar powder
- 1/4 cup cocoa powder
- 1 cup all-purpose flour
- 1 large egg
- 3/4 ounce of the milk

Instructions:

1. Turn the temperature up to 350 degrees. Spray two donut pans, each with a capacity of six, with nonstick cooking spray.
2. Flour, cocoa powder, baking powder, and salt should be mixed together in a bowl of medium size.
3. Sugar and egg should be mixed together in a small bowl and whisked until the mixture is fluffy and light. Add milk and vanilla and whisk until smooth.
4. Stir the wet ingredients into the dry ingredients until combined, but be careful not to overmix the ingredients. Combine the chocolate chips with the other ingredients.
5. One can use a spoon to transfer the mixture into the donut molds that have been prepared. It is important to fill each donut mold almost entirely.
6. Bake donuts at 350 for 8-10 minutes until done.
7. Take the donuts out of the oven and place them on a paper towel or a kitchen towel to prevent them from becoming soggy while they are still in the pan. Donuts should be allowed to cool for a minute or two, during which time they should be flipped over once.
8. Glaze requires some mixing. If one wants, one can either completely submerge each donut in glaze or drizzle it on top.
9. Enjoy while it's still warm!

Nutritional Info:

Calories: 134 kcal Fat: 2 g Protein: 3 g Carbs: 27 g Sugar: 17 g Sodium: 111 mg

81. Strawberry Ice cream

Prep Time: 5 minutes

Cook Time: 35 minutes

Servings: 6

Ingredients:

- 2 tbsp fresh lemon juice
- 1 pound of fresh strawberries
- 1/3 of a cup of honey
- 1 cup of unsweetened almond milk i
- 1 egg white

Instructions:

1. Put all of the ingredients in a blender and mix them together until the strawberries are completely combined.

2. The mixture should be poured into a bowl of a frozen ice cream maker that has been inserted into the machine. Turn the mixture over for thirty to thirty-five minutes or until it reaches the consistency of soft-serve ice cream.

3. One can serve it at this point, but keep in mind that it will be on the softer side. Transfer to a container that is safe to be placed in the freezer, and freeze for approximately one hour. It will have a more authentic ice cream texture when scooped.

4. Consuming this within the first hour will yield the best results; however, one can store it in the freezer for up to one month if one covers the surface with some plastic wrap to prevent it from becoming freezer burned. It will turn into solid ice. When one is ready to serve, remove the frozen dessert from the freezer and allow it to thaw for about twenty to thirty minutes before scooping. It will have the consistency of shaved ice but will be creamier, and it will still be delicious!

Nutritional Info:

Calories: 92 kcal Fat: 1 g Protein: 1 g Carbs: 22 g Sugar: 19 g Sodium: 1 mg

82. Chocolate Truffles

Prep Time: 30 minutes

Cook Time: 30 minutes

Servings: 22

Ingredients:

- ⅛ teaspoon Salt
- 2 teaspoons of vanilla extract
- 1/4 cup Unsweetened cocoa powder
- 1 1/2 cups of condensed milk
- 1 1/4 cups Protein Powder

Instructions:

1. Condensed milk and stevia extract should be mixed together in a large bowl using a whisk.
2. Mix the cocoa powder, protein powder, and salt into the bowl. Mix together using a whisk until everything is evenly distributed (the mixture should thicken like frosting). Cover and chill the mixture for at least 5 hours in the refrigerator (the mixture should firm up).
3. Using parchment paper, line a baking sheet for the cookies.
4. To portion the fudge onto the cookie sheet, use a cookie. Keep covered in the refrigerator for thirty minutes to one hour.
5. After one has formed balls from the scoops by rolling them between the palms, place them back in the refrigerator for another half an hour to an hour. Serve, and have fun with it!

Nutritional Info:

Calories: 50 kcal Fat: 2.5 g Protein: 6 g Carbs: 2 g Sugar: 0.25 g Sodium: 45 mg

83. Chocolate Amaretti

Prep Time: 5 minutes

Cook Time: 15 minutes

Servings: 8

Ingredients:

- ½ teaspoon baking powder
- 1/2 teaspoon of almond extract
- 2 tablespoon cocoa powder

- 1 egg white
- ⅓ cup powdered sweetener
- 1/4 cup of powdered sugar
- 1 cup of ground almond flour
- A pinch of salt

Instructions:

1. Prepare a cookie sheet by lining it with parchment paper and preheating the oven to 180C electric/350F/160C fan temperature.
2. Sift the powdered sweetener to remove any lumps that may have formed. After that, combine all of the dry ingredients by stirring them together: cocoa powder, almond flour, sweetener, baking powder, and a little bit of salt.
3. In a separate bowl, whip the white eggs until it forms glossy peaks. Mix in the vanilla and almond extracts until combined.
4. Mix the wet and dry ingredients together using a spatula, continuing to stir until a smooth batter is formed.
5. Roll the dough into a ball and cut it into quarters. From a quarter of the dough, roll two balls and place them on the cookie sheet that has been prepared, slightly flattening them.
6. Bake the cookies for approximately 13 to 15 minutes or until cracks begin to appear on the tops.
7. After the cookies have had a chance to cool slightly, sprinkle them with powdered sweetener.

Nutritional Info:

Calories: 80 kcal Fat: 7 g Protein: 3 g Carbs: 3 g Sugar: 0.6 g Sodium: 12 mg

84. Chocolate Covered Strawberries

Prep Time: 5 minutes

Cook Time: 50 minutes

Servings: 3

Ingredients:

- 1 teaspoon of avocado oil

- 3 ounces of dark chocolate
- 12 large strawberries

Instructions:

1. Apply wax paper to line a plate or a tray.
2. After being washed, the strawberries should be dried off using a paper towel.
3. Put the chocolate chips in a bowl that can be heated in the microwave. They should be melted in the microwave using intervals of 30 seconds, with stirring after each interval. After three of these sessions, they ought to have melted to a significant degree.
4. Combine the oil with the melted chocolate by stirring it.
5. Coat each strawberry in the melted chocolate and set them to the side. To remove any excess chocolate, lift it up and rotate it clockwise to remove it. Position on the melted wax paper.
6. Put the strawberries into the refrigerator for about half an hour before serving them.

Nutritional Info:

Calories: 107 kcal Fat: 6 g Protein: 2 g Carbs: 9 g Sugar: 5 g Sodium: 0.6 mg

85. Greek Yogurt Brownies

Prep Time: 10 minutes

Cook Time: 25 minutes

Servings: 16

Ingredients:

- 1/2 teaspoon of Baking soda
- 1/4 teaspoon of Salt
- 1 teaspoon of cornstarch
- 2 tablespoons of coconut oil
- 1/2 cup of cocoa powder
- 1/4 Cup of Coconut sugar
- 2/3 cup of non-fat Greek yogurt
- 2 Large eggs
- 5 ounces of dark chocolate

Instructions:

1. Prepare a pan with parchment paper that is 8 inches by 8 inches, and preheat the oven to 325 degrees.
2. Whisk the yogurt, sugar, and eggs together in a large bowl until combined.
3. Put the oil and 4 ounces of the chocolate into a small bowl that can go in the microwave and heat it until it's melted and smooth, which should take about a minute. Stir into the egg mixture using a whisk.
4. Mix the cocoa powder, cornstarch, soda, and salt together with a whisk. After that, break up the remaining chocolate into small pieces and stir it in.
5. Spread the mixture into the prepared pan, then place it in the oven and bake for about 22 to 23 minutes, or until a fork stabbed in the center comes out clean. Immediately place the bowls in the refrigerator and leave them there for 15 minutes. After that, take it off the heat and let it finish cooling down on the counter.
6. Cut it up, and eat it up!

Nutritional Info:

Calories: 103 kcal Fat: 6 g Protein: 3 g Carbs: 10 g Sugar: 8 g Sodium: 52 mg

Chapter 8: Snack Recipes

86. Guacamole with Bell Pepper Dippers

Prep Time: 5 minutes

Cook Time: 1 minute

Servings: 1

Ingredients:

- 1 teaspoon pepitas
- ¼ cup guacamole
- 1 cup sliced bell peppers

Instructions:

1. Serve bell pepper slices with the guacamole, then sprinkle with pepitas.

Nutritional Info:

Calories: 123 kcal Fat: 7 g Protein: 3 g Carbs: 11 g Sugar: 5 g Sodium: 290 mg

87. Cottage Cheese with Fruit

Prep Time: 2 minutes

Cook Time: 2 minutes

Servings: 1

Ingredients:

- ½ cup of peach
- ¼ cup of mandarin
- ¼ cup of pineapple
- 1 cup of cottage cheese

Instructions:

1. After removing the juice from the oranges, pineapple, and peaches, place the fruit in a modest bowl.
2. Combine the fruit in the bowl.
3. Add cottage cheese as a topping.

Nutritional Info:

Calories: 366 kcal Fat: 10 g Protein: 25 g Carbs: 40 g Sugar: 35 g Sodium: 766 mg

88. Celery Sticks with Cream Cheese

Prep Time: 10 minutes

Cook Time: 0 minutes

Servings: 4

Ingredients:

- ½ cup mayonnaise
- 1 cup shredded mozzarella cheese
- 1 block of cream cheese
- 1 package of Italian dressing mix

- 6 or 7 stalks of celery

Instructions:

1. Separate each stalk of celery into three equal pieces. Set aside.
2. Combine mozzarella cheese, cream cheese, Italian dressing mix, and mayonnaise in a mixing bowl.
3. Fill the celery with the cream cheese and butter mixture.
4. If one so wants, sprinkle dried parsley and paprika over the celery before serving. Keep chilled in the refrigerator until ready to serve.

Nutritional Info:

Calories: 293 kcal Fat: 11 g Protein: 8 g Carbs: 44 g Sugar: 0.1 g Sodium: 333 mg

89. Cucumber with Hummus

Prep Time: 15 minutes

Cook Time: 0 minutes

Servings: 3

Ingredients:

- 1 cucumber

- 9 cherry tomatoes
- 1/2 a cup of hummus
- ¼ cup feta cheese crumbled
- Pinch of fresh parsley.
- Pinch of salt and pepper

Instructions:

1. The cucumbers and tomatoes should both be washed and dried.
2. Cut the tomato in half and slice the cucumber into thin rounds about an eighth of an inch thick.
3. On each slice of cucumber, spread about a teaspoon's worth of hummus.
4. On top of each slice, place one-half of the tomato halves.
5. Crumbled feta cheese and chopped fresh parsley should be sprinkled on top. Add salt and pepper to taste.

Nutritional Info:

Calories: 20 kcal Fat: 1 g Protein: 1 g Carbs: 3 g Sugar: 1 g Sodium: 2 mg

90. Olives with Feta Cheese

Prep Time: 5 minutes

Cook Time: 5 minutes

Servings: 1

Ingredients:

- 1 teaspoon red pepper flakes
- 1/2 teaspoon dried oregano
- 3 tablespoons of olive oil
- 1 cup olives
- 3 ounces of feta cheese

Instructions:

1. Put all of the ingredients into a small bowl and blend them thoroughly with a good mix. At the very least, olives should be given twenty minutes of marinating time before being enjoyed.

Nutritional Info:

Calories: 25 kcal Fat: 2 g Protein: 1 g Carbs: 0 g Sugar: 0 g Sodium: 230 mg

91. Roasted Chickpeas

Prep Time: 5 minutes

Cook Time: 20 minutes

Servings: 1

Ingredients:

- 1 teaspoon of paprika
- 1 teaspoon of curry powder
- 2 tablespoons of olive oil
- 1 1/2 cups of cooked chickpeas

Instructions:

1. Prepare a large baking sheet by lining it with parchment paper and preheating the oven to 425 degrees Fahrenheit.
2. Place the chickpeas on a clean dish towel and use another towel to blot them dry. Take off aany loose skins.
3. Place the dry chickpeas on the baking sheet and sprinkle them with several generous pinches of salt and a drizzle of olive oil before placing them in the oven.
4. Roast the chickpeas in the oven for twenty to thirty minutes or until they are crisp and golden brown. Since different ovens produce varying results, if the chickpeas are not crispy enough, continue cooking them until they are.
5. Take the chickpeas out of the oven, and if one is going to use any spices, toss them with a few pinches of those spices while they're still warm.
6. Keep roasted chickpeas at room temperature in a container with a lid that is only slightly secure. It is preferable to use them within the next two days.

Nutritional Info:

Calories: 153 kcal Fat: 3 g Protein: 7 g Carbs: 25 g Sugar: 4 g Sodium: 90 mg

92. Turkey Roll-Ups

Prep Time: 10 minutes

Cook Time: 5 minutes

Servings: 4

Ingredients:

- 2 teaspoons Dijon Mustard
- 2 teaspoons of honey
- 1/3 of whole red pepper
- 1/4 of a big English cucumber
- 2 large leaves of red leaf lettuce
- 8 pieces of turkey breast

- 8 big basil leaves

Instructions:

1. Honey and Dijon mustard should be mixed together in a small bowl until they are completely incorporated.

2. Place one turkey slice at a time on a plate or chopping board. Spread about a half teaspoon's worth of the honey-mustard mixture along the width of the turkey slice, beginning about two inches from one end of the slice. Put a piece of lettuce on top, followed by a couple of cucumber sticks and some red pepper slices, and then place another piece of lettuce on top of that. After that, place a basil leaf on top, and then roll everything up in the turkey slice.

Nutritional Info:

Calories: 41 kcal Fat: 1 g Protein: 4 g Carbs: 5 g Sugar: 5 g Sodium: 222 mg

93. Hard Boiled Eggs

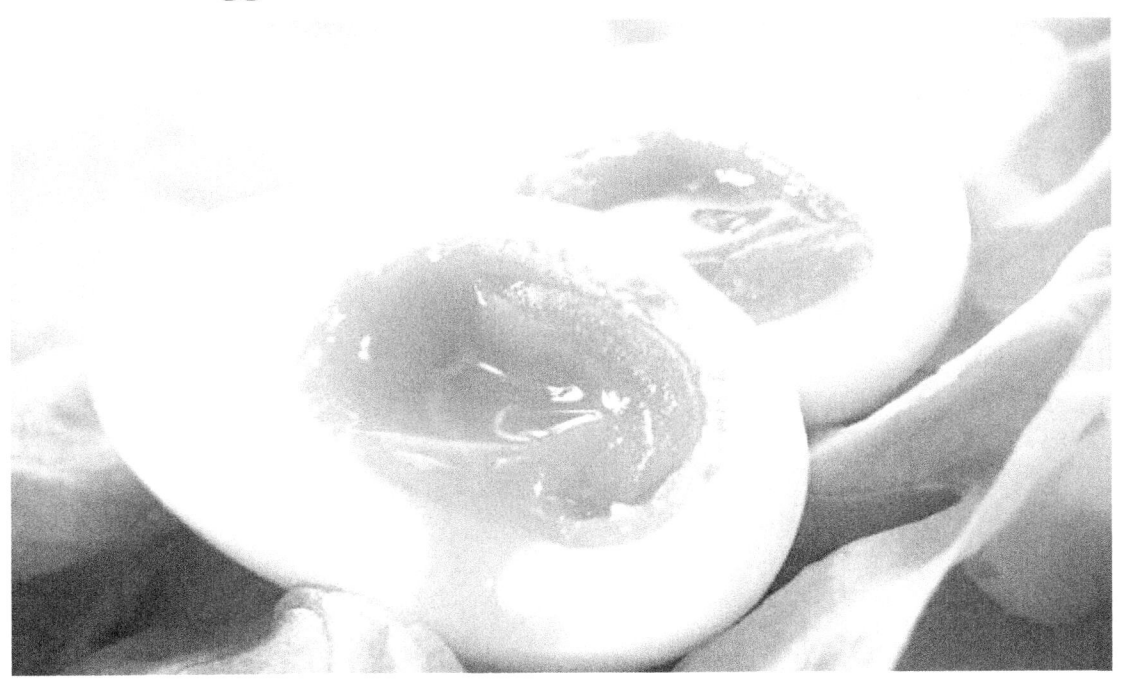

Prep Time: 2 minutes

Cook Time: 10 minutes

Servings: 1

Ingredients:

- 3 Eggs

- Pinch of Salt
- Pinch of Pepper
- Bottle of Water
- 1 cup of Ice cubes

Instructions:

1. Take a saucepan and fill it with water.
2. In the saucepan, add 3 eggs and let them boil at the full flame for 10 minutes.
3. Take the flame off and transfer the eggs to a bowl with water and ice cubes.
4. Take a spoon and crack the eggs. Remove its shell and serve with and sprinkle of salt and pepper.

Nutritional Info:

Calories: 78 kcal Fat: 5 g Protein: 6 g Carbs: 1 g Sugar: 1 g Sodium: 70 mg

94. Apple with Peanut Butter

Prep Time: 5 minutes

Cook Time: 0 minutes

Servings: 1

Ingredients:

- 2 big apples
- 1 cup of peanut butter

Instructions:

1. Cut the apple into equal small slices and serve with peanut butter.

Nutritional Info:

Calories: 95 kcal Fat: 2 g Protein: 0 g Carbs: 25 g Sugar: 15 g Sodium: 70 mg

95. Carrot Chips

Prep Time: 5 minutes

Cook Time: 20 minutes

Servings: 2

Ingredients:

- ½ teaspoon of dry parsley
- ⅓ teaspoon of salt
- ½ teaspoon garlic powder
- 2 tablespoons of avocado oil
- 4 medium carrots

Instructions:

1. Prepare the oven to 425 degrees Fahrenheit. Prepare a baking sheet by lining it with aluminum foil and setting it aside.
2. Carrot slices should be tossed in oil, garlic powder, chopped parsley, and salt in a large bowl until the carrots are equally covered with the ingredients.
3. Place the carrot slices on the baking sheet that has been prepared in a single layer. Be careful

not to crowd the baking sheet too much.

4. After 20 to 25 minutes in the oven, or when the edges are beginning to brown, remove from the oven.

Nutritional Info:

Calories: 155 kcal Fat: 13 g Protein: 0 g Carbs: 7 g Sugar: 15 g Sodium: 437 mg

BONUS 1: 40-Day Meal Plan

Remember that in the first phases you will need to eat only liquid and then semiliquids. This meal plean is meant to help you when you will be able to eat traditional solid food, and has been created to help you with well calculated nutritional values, so that you can swap any kind of meal.

Day 1

Breakfast: Blueberry Breakfast Pancakes (Recipe 11)

Lunch: Mushroom Alfredo Cauliflower Gnocchi (Recipe 26)

Snack: Guacamole with Bell Pepper Dippers (Recipe 86)

Dinner: Birria (Recipe 56)

Dessert: Black Bean Fudge Brownies (Recipe 71)

Day 2

Breakfast: Cottage Cheese Breakfast Bowl (Recipe 12)

Lunch: Cauliflower Pizza Crust (Recipe 27)

Snack: Cottage Cheese with Fruit (Recipe 87)

Dinner: Seafood Enchiladas (Recipe 47)

Dessert: Zucchini Double Chocolate Bread (Recipe 72)

Day 3

Breakfast: Scrambled Eggs with Cottage Cheese (Recipe 13)

Lunch: Mushroom Risotto (Recipe 28)

Snack: Celery Sticks with Cream Cheese (Recipe 88)

Dinner: Beef Stroganoff (Recipe 57)

Dessert: Chocolate Tahini Cookies (Recipe 73)

Day 4

Breakfast: Banana Muffins (Recipe 14)

Lunch: Vegetable Lasagna (Recipe 29)

Snack: Cucumber with Hummus (Recipe 89)

Dinner: Stuffed Chicken Breast (Recipe 69)

Dessert: Oatmeal and Peanut Butter Cookies (Recipe 74)

Day 5

Breakfast: Egg Salad (Recipe 15)

Lunch: Stuffed Peppers (Recipe 30)

Snack: Olives with Feta Cheese (Recipe 90)

Dinner: Creamy Tuscan Chicken (Recipe 58)

Dessert: Sweet and Sour Potato Muffins (Recipe 75)

Day 6

Breakfast: Tuna and Spinach Pancakes (Recipe 16)

Lunch: Pan Quesadilla with Jalapeno Ranch (Recipe 31)

Snack: Roasted Chickpeas (Recipe 91)

Dinner: Pumpkin Chilli Chicken (Recipe 68)

Dessert: Chai Tea Glaze with Pumpkin Spice Bundtlettes (Recipe 76)

Day 7

Breakfast: Baked Eggs with Greens and Beans (Recipe 17)

Lunch: Vegetarian Chili (Recipe 32)

Snack: Turkey Roll Ups (Recipe 92)

Dinner: Gyro Meat (Recipe 59)

Dessert: Avocado Brownies with Frosting (Recipe 77)

Day 8

Breakfast: Apple Cinnamon Porridge (Recipe 18)

Lunch: Stir Fry Tofu with Peanut Sauce (Recipe 33)

Snack: Hard Boiled Eggs (Recipe 93)

Dinner: Fish Curry (Recipe 54)

Dessert: Fluff Cake (Recipe 78)

Day 9

Breakfast: Strawberry Avocado Smoothie (Recipe 19)

Lunch: Vegetarian Meatballs (Recipe 34)

Snack: Apple with Peanut Butter (Recipe 94)

Dinner: White Sauce Breast Chicken (Recipe 60)

Dessert: Vegan Chocolate Pudding (Recipe 79)

Day 10

Breakfast: Green Vegetable Fritters (Recipe 20)

Lunch: Tofu Lettuce Wraps (Recipe 35)

Snack: Carrot Chips (Recipe 95)

Dinner: Tuna, White Bean and Dill Salad (Recipe 53)

Dessert: Chocolate Baked Donuts (Recipe 80)

Day 11

Breakfast: Apple Cheese Strudel (Recipe 21)

Lunch: Creamy Zucchini Pasta (Recipe 36)

Snack: Guacamole with Bell Pepper Dippers (Recipe 86)

Dinner: Beef and Broccoli Stir Fry (Recipe 61)

Dessert: Strawberry Ice cream (Recipe 81)

Day 12

Breakfast: Vegetable Breakfast Bakes (Recipe 22)

Lunch: Green Curry Buddha Bowl (Recipe 37)

Snack: Cottage Cheese with Fruit (Recipe 87)

Dinner: Fish and Shrimp Stew (Recipe 45)

Dessert: Chocolate Truffles (Recipe 82)

Day 13

Breakfast: Fat Burning Smoothie (Recipe 23)

Lunch: Burrito Bowl with Avocado Crema (Recipe 38)

Snack: Celery Sticks with Cream Cheese (Recipe 88)

Dinner: Chicken Pot Pie (Recipe 64)

Dessert: Chocolate Amaretti (Recipe 83)

Day 14

Breakfast: Chia Pudding (Recipe 24)

Lunch: Sesame Garlic Ramen Noodles (Recipe 39)

Snack: Cucumber with Hummus (Recipe 89)

Dinner: (Recipe)

Dessert: Chocolate Covered Strawberries (Recipe 84)

Day 15

Breakfast: Cranberry and Raspberry Smoothie (Recipe 25)

Lunch: Cauliflower Taco with Avocado Crema (Recipe 40)

Snack: Olives with Feta Cheese (Recipe 90)

Dinner: Meatloaf with Vegetables (Recipe 62)

Dessert: Greek Yogurt Brownies (Recipe 85)

Day 16

Breakfast: Blueberry Breakfast Pancakes (Recipe 11)

Lunch: Mushroom Alfredo Cauliflower Gnocchi (Recipe 26)

Snack: Roasted Chickpeas (Recipe 91)

Dinner: Tomato Chicken Curry with Cauliflower Rice (Recipe 65)

Dessert: Black Bean Fudge Brownies (Recipe 71)

Day 17

Breakfast: Cottage Cheese Breakfast Bowl (Recipe 12)

Lunch: Cauliflower Pizza Crust (Recipe 27)

Snack: Turkey Roll Ups (Recipe 92)

Dinner: Spinach and Turkey Lasagna (Recipe 63)

Dessert: Zucchini Double Chocolate Bread (Recipe 72)

Day 18

Breakfast: Scrambled Eggs with Cottage Cheese (Recipe 13)

Lunch: Mushroom Risotto (Recipe 28)

Snack: Hard Boiled Eggs (Recipe 93)

Dinner: Birria (Recipe 56)

Dessert: Chocolate Tahini Cookies (Recipe 73)

Day 19

Breakfast: Banana Muffins (Recipe 14)

Lunch: Vegetable Lasagna (Recipe 29)

Snack: Apple with Peanut Butter (Recipe 94)

Dinner: Palco Tomato Chicken Curry with Cauliflower Rice (Recipe 65)

Dessert: Oatmeal and Peanut Butter Cookies (Recipe 74)

Day 20

Breakfast: Egg Salad (Recipe 15)

Lunch: Stuffed Peppers (Recipe 30)

Snack: Carrot Chips (Recipe 95)

Dinner: Balacao Guisado (Recipe 50)

Dessert: Sweet and Sour Potato Muffins (Recipe 75)

Day 21

    Breakfast: Tuna and Spinach Pancakes (Recipe 16)

    Lunch: Pan Quesadilla with Jalapeno Ranch (Recipe 31)

    Snack: Guacamole with Bell Pepper Dippers (Recipe 86)

    Dinner: Tandoori Chicken (Recipe 66)

    Dessert: Chai Tea Glaze with Pumpkin Spice Bundtlettes (Recipe 76)

Day 22

    Breakfast: Baked Eggs with Greens and Beans (Recipe 17)

    Lunch: Vegetarian Chili (Recipe 32)

    Snack: Cottage Cheese with Fruit (Recipe 87)

    Dinner: Shrimp and Cauliflower Bake (Recipe 44)

    Dessert: Avocado Brownies with Frosting (Recipe 77)

Day 23

    Breakfast: Apple Cinnamon Porridge (Recipe 18)

    Lunch: Stir Fry Tofu with Peanut Sauce (Recipe 33)

    Snack: Celery Sticks with Cream Cheese (Recipe 89)

    Dinner: Shiitake Mushroom Chicken Ramen (Recipe 67)

    Dessert: Fluff Cake (Recipe 78)

Day 24

    Breakfast: Strawberry Avocado Smoothie (Recipe 19)

    Lunch: Vegetarian Meatballs (Recipe 34)

    Snack: Cucumber with Hummus (Recipe 86)

    Dinner: Panko and Parmesan Crusted Scallops (Recipe 46)

    Dessert: Vegan Chocolate Pudding (Recipe 79)

Day 25

Breakfast: Green Vegetable Fritters (Recipe 20)

Lunch: Tofu Lettuce Wraps (Recipe 35)

Snack: Olives with Feta Cheese (Recipe 90)

Dinner: Pumpkin Chilli Chicken (Recipe 68)

Dessert: Chocolate Baked Donuts (Recipe 80)

Day 26

Breakfast: Apple Cheese Strudel (Recipe 21)

Lunch: Creamy Zucchini Pasta (Recipe 36)

Snack: Roasted Chickpeas (Recipe 91)

Dinner: Shrimp and Corn Succotash (Recipe 42)

Dessert: Strawberry Ice cream (Recipe 81)

Day 27

Breakfast: Vegetable Breakfast Bakes (Recipe 22)

Lunch: Green Curry Buddha Bowl (Recipe 37)

Snack: Turkey Roll Ups (Recipe 92)

Dinner: Creamy Mushroom Chicken (Recipe 70)

Dessert: Chocolate Truffles (Recipe 82)

Day 28

Breakfast: Fat Burning Smoothie (Recipe 23)

Lunch: Burrito Bowl with Avocado Crema (Recipe 38)

Snack: Hard Boiled Eggs (Recipe 93)

Dinner: Korean Grilled Mackerel (Recipe 52)

Dessert: Chocolate Amaretti (Recipe 83)

Day 28

    Breakfast: Fat Burning Smoothie (Recipe 23)

    Lunch: Burrito Bowl with Avocado Crema (Recipe 38)

    Snack: Hard Boiled Eggs (Recipe 93)

    Dinner: Korean Grilled Mackerel (Recipe 52)

    Dessert: Chocolate Amaretti (Recipe 83)

Day 29

    Breakfast: Cottage Cheese Breakfast Bowl (Recipe 12)

    Lunch: Pan Quesadilla with Jalapeno Ranch (Recipe 31)

    Snack: Guacamole with Bell Pepper Dippers (Recipe 86)

    Dinner: Chicken Pot Pie (Recipe 64)

    Dessert: Sweet and Sour Potato Muffins (Recipe 75)

Day 30

    Breakfast: Banana Muffins (Recipe 14)

    Lunch: Burrito Bowl with Avocado Crema (Recipe 38)

    Snack: Apple with Peanut Butter (Recipe 94)

    Dinner: Tuna, White Bean and Dill Salad (Recipe 53)

    Dessert: Black Bean Fudge Brownies (Recipe 71)

Day 31

    Breakfast: Strawberry Avocado Smoothie (Recipe 19)

    Lunch: Cauliflower Pizza Crust (Recipe 27)

    Snack: Roasted Chickpeas (Recipe 91)

    Dinner: Stuffed Chicken Breast (Recipe 69)

    Dessert: Chocolate Baked Donuts (Recipe 80)

Day 32

    Breakfast: Scrambled Eggs with Cottage Cheese (Recipe 13)

    Lunch: Tofu Lettuce Wraps (Recipe 35)

    Snack: Olives with Feta Cheese (Recipe 90)

    Dinner: Gyro Meat (Recipe 59)

Dessert: Strawberry Ice cream (Recipe 81)

Day 33

Breakfast: Tuna and Spinach Pancakes (Recipe 16)

Lunch: Stuffed Peppers (Recipe 30)

Snack: Cottage Cheese with Fruit (Recipe 87)

Dinner: Creamy Tuscan Chicken (Recipe 58)

Dessert: Zucchini Double Chocolate Bread (Recipe 72)

Day 34

Breakfast: Egg Salad (Recipe 15)

Lunch: Burrito Bowl with Avocado Crema (Recipe 38)

Snack: Cucumber with Hummus (Recipe 89)

Dinner: White Sauce Breast Chicken (Recipe 60)

Dessert: Sweet and Sour Potato Muffins (Recipe 75)

Day 35

Breakfast: Baked Eggs with Greens and Beans (Recipe 17)

Lunch: Cauliflower Taco with Avocado Crema (Recipe 40)

Snack: Celery Sticks with Cream Cheese (Recipe 89)

Dinner: Shrimp and Cauliflower Bake (Recipe 44)

Dessert: Chocolate Truffles (Recipe 82)

Day 36

Breakfast: Apple Cinnamon Porridge (Recipe 18)

Lunch: Tofu Lettuce Wraps (Recipe 35)

Snack: Hard Boiled Eggs (Recipe 93)

Dinner: Birria (Recipe 56)

Dessert: Black Bean Fudge Brownies (Recipe 71)

Day 37

Breakfast: Blueberry Breakfast Pancakes (Recipe 11)

Lunch: Pan Quesadilla with Jalapeno Ranch (Recipe 31)

Snack: Guacamole with Bell Pepper Dippers (Recipe 86)

Dinner: Beef Stroganoff (Recipe 57)

Dessert: Balacao Guisado (Recipe 50)

Day 38

Breakfast: Cottage Cheese Breakfast Bowl (Recipe 12)

Lunch: Vegetable Lasagna (Recipe 29)

Snack: Hard Boiled Eggs (Recipe 93)

Dinner: Paleo Tomato Chicken Curry with Cauliflower Rice (Recipe 65)

Dessert: Chocolate Tahini Cookies (Recipe 73)

Day 39

Breakfast: Strawberry Avocado Smoothie (Recipe 19)

Lunch: Stir Fry Tofu with Peanut Sauce (Recipe 33)

Snack: Celery Sticks with Cream Cheese (Recipe 89)

Dinner: Fish and Shrimp Stew (Recipe 45)

Dessert: Chocolate Tahini Cookies (Recipe 73)

Day 40

Breakfast: Baked Eggs with Greens and Beans (Recipe 17)

Lunch: Vegetarian Meatballs (Recipe 34)

Snack: Turkey Roll Ups (Recipe 92)

Dinner: Tuna, White Bean and Dill Salad (Recipe 53)

Dessert: Chocolate Amaretti (Recipe 83)

Conclusion

The gastric sleeve procedure is a weight loss treatment that is risk-free and supported by clinical evidence. The operation includes severing the connection between the fundus, the upper section of the stomach, and the remainder of the organ to reduce the stomach size. If the stomach is smaller, one will naturally have less appetite. Because of this, one is less likely to consume excessive food because one feels full sooner.

A sleeve gastrectomy, also referred to as a vertical sleeve gastrectomy, is a surgical treatment used to aid with weight loss. Laparoscopic surgery, in which several tiny incisions are made in the patient's upper abdomen to accommodate the insertion of a camera and surgical equipment, is the method of choice for carrying out this procedure. A sleeve gastrectomy involves removing around 80% of the stomach, leaving behind an approximation of the size and contour of a banana in the form of a tube-shaped stomach.

If one reduces the size of their stomach, they can ingest only a certain amount of food at one time. In addition, the surgery causes hormonal shifts that are beneficial to weight loss and help speed up the process. These same hormonal shifts assist in alleviating diseases such as high blood pressure and heart disease associated with being overweight.

Sleeve gastrectomy has been shown to result in sustained weight loss. The weight one loses is directly proportional to the changes one makes to their lifestyle. Within two years, one should be able to shed at least sixty percent of their excess weight, if not even more.

In addition to causing weight loss, sleeve gastrectomy has the potential to alleviate or even cure several illnesses that are linked to obesity, including the following:

- Cardiovascular disease
- Unhealthy levels of blood pressure
- Poor cholesterol management
- Obstructive sleep apnea
- Type 2 diabetes
- Stroke
- Infertility

After surgery, the patient will only be allowed to consume clear liquids for the first week after the procedure. In addition to water, one can consume clear broth, beverages without caffeine, and sugar-free variations of various drink combinations such as Kool-Aid and Crystal Light. Avoid anything with added sugar, carbonation, or caffeine. Carbonated beverages are especially bad.

The post-operative diet will begin to include more substantial liquids once the first week has passed. Applesauce, cream of wheat, Greek yogurt, protein smoothies, sugar-free ice creams and puddings are some foods that could fall into this category.

BONUS 2 - Handy Conversion chart

COOKING CONVERSION CHART

WEIGHT

IMPERIAL	METRIC
1/2 oz	15 g
1 oz	29 g
2 oz	57 g
3 oz	85 g
4 oz	113 g
5 oz	141 g
6 oz	170 g
8 oz	227 g
10 oz	283 g
12 oz	340 g
13 oz	369 g
14 oz	397 g
15 oz	425 g
1 lb	453 g

TEMPERATURE

FAHRENHEIT	CELSIUS
100 °F	37 °C
150 °F	65 °C
200 °F	93 °C
250 °F	121 °C
300 °F	150 °C
325 °F	160 °C
350 °F	180 °C
375 °F	190 °C
400 °F	200 °C
425 °F	220 °C
450 °F	230 °C
500 °F	260 °C
525 °F	274 °C
550 °F	288 °C

MEASUREMENT

CUP	ONCES	MILLILITERS	TBSP
8 cup	64 oz	1895 ml	128
6 cup	48 oz	1420 ml	96
5 cup	40 oz	1180 ml	80
4 cup	32 oz	960 ml	64
2 cup	16 oz	500 ml	32
1 cup	8 oz	250 ml	16
3/4 cup	6 oz	177 ml	12
2/3 cup	5 oz	158 ml	11
1/2 cup	4 oz	118 ml	8
3/8 cup	3 oz	90 ml	6
1/3 cup	2.5 oz	79 ml	5.5
1/4 cup	2 oz	59 ml	4
1/8 cup	1 oz	30 ml	3
1/16 cup	1/2 oz	15 ml	1

Printed in Great Britain
by Amazon